Feedback

One of the highlights of these books is the attention to detail, small and large regarding the physical locations and descriptions given by Joe (McMoneagle). *Reading the* (execution) *Market Square data for example, was like being transported to the actual site. These are the little gems of information Remote Viewing can surprise us with from time to time. Quite remarkable indeed.*

Personally I found your details on history of Joan of Arc fascinating. I had heard of her of course, but I had never delved into the real story.

The depiction of (French King) *Charles VII appears to be spot on.*

Naturally, there was a regret that we have no reliable contemporary portrait (of Joan)*, but I wrote it off as an unfortunate fact. Then the surprise comes -- we have Joe with two "pictures" that history does not have - the sketch of Joan at the pillar (not stake) and finally that beautiful drawing of her face.*

I found the Joan of Arc book fascinating. The added information provided by Joe was just terrific, and consistent with the rest of what I have seen via your books. In Joan, as in Otzi, there is a wealth of new information...

After I read the Joan of Arc material, I wanted to read more about Medieval history.

Have read the Joan of Arc book and loved it, amazing. As I was reading through the Execution Square chapter, I felt I was in the square, as the description really takes the reader straight to the place. Never really would have thought someone may have given Joan something to take the edge off such a cruel demise. Really thought provoking, as the church and politics doesn't change much, just gets cloudier. Just about to start Titanic, then happy to purchase Amelia book. Thanks for the great read, and again will be soon to order... Thanks for the great books, keep finding the great mysteries.

As time goes on others will get word and pick up the book(s).

The Quick Take

Authority to award the Legion of Merit Medal is reserved for general officers and flag officers in pay grade O-9 (e.g., Lieutenant General and Vice Admiral) and above... https://en.wikipedia.org/ wiki/ Legion_of_Merit

At least two witnesses must submit seven military forms for consideration as to the proper award. Based on the quality of the information, the military's Decorations Personnel selected the medal with the following prerequisites:

The award is given for service rendered in a clearly exceptional manner. For service not related to actual war the term "key individual" applies to a narrower range of positions than in time of war and requires evidence of significant achievement. In peacetime, service should be in the nature of a special requirement or of an extremely difficult duty performed in an unprecedented and clearly exceptional manner.

During his career, Mr. McMoneagle has provided ...informational support to the Central Intelligence Agency (CIA), Defense Intelligence Agency (DIA), National Security Agency (NSA), Drug Enforcement Agency (DEA), Secret Service, Federal Bureau of Investigation (FBI), United States Customs (ICE),the National Security Council (NSC), most major commands (Army, Navy, Air Force, Intelligence) within the Department of Defense (DOD), and hundreds of other individuals, companies, and corporations.

Paragraph from Mr. McMoneagle's CV.

This whole *Evidential Details Mystery Series* received Five Stars from Good Reads.com, and Book Wire awarded Five Stars to the Amelia Earhart and Otzi the Iceman books. They did not read the other volumes.

The

Evidential Details Mystery Series

Decorated United States Military Intelligence Psychic
Remote Viewer solves some of History's Greatest Mysteries

U.S. Army Legion of Merit Medal

Joan of Arc
At the Stake

Seeds/McMoneagle

©2020

The Logistics News Network, LLC. Chicago, Illinois

Medals Received

Legion of Merit   Meritorious Service

Citations

Meritorious Service with **one** Oak Leaf Cluster;[1]
Army Commendation with **two** Oak Leaf Clusters, Presidential Unit;
Meritorious Unit with **three** Oak Leaf Clusters;
Vietnam Gallantry Cross with Palm for gathering enemy intelligence for
Allied counter offensives.

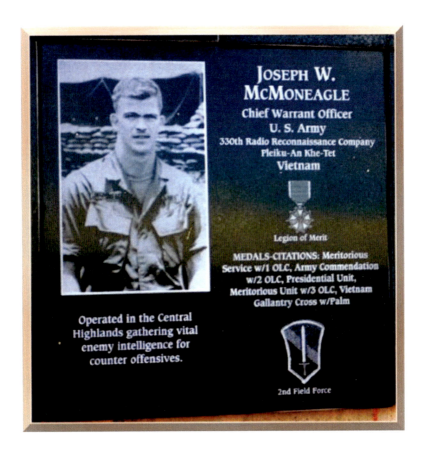

The Commemorative Military Plaque on the Brick Wall

In what is clearly the most fascinating component of U.S. Military History, Joseph McMoneagle is the only man to be awarded medals for consistent accuracy in Remote Viewing (Psy-functioning) by a military. As *Operation Star Gate's* Number 1 Military Intelligence asset, he was the Pentagon's go to man when secret data could not be obtained by any other means or was time sensitive.

The Evidential Details Imprint is a
Division of the Logistics News Network, LLC.

RV Session Work ©2001 All rights reserved
Updated Book Edition ©2020 by LNN, llc.

The Evidential Details Mysteries Series

Joan of Arc – At the Stake, includes biographical references.
ISBN: 978-0-9826928-3–7

Joan of Arc (1412-1431) – Joan of Arc Trial Transcripts – French Medieval History - French Military History – 100 Years War - Bishop Pierre Cauchon – French King Charles VII – City of Rouen - European Medieval Executions - British Military History – English King Henry V – Battle of Agincourt – The Vatican - Pope Benedict XV - McMoneagle, Joseph – Puthoff PhD., Dr. Harold E. – Remote Viewing – Stanford Research Institute – Neurophysiology - Anomalous Cognition

Library of Congress Card Number: 2010904636

Book design by Logistics News Network, llc.
Printed in the United States of America

If you are unable to purchase this, or our other history books in your local bookstore, visit our web site at **www.EvidentialDetails.com**

Table of Contents

Part Two

Part Three

ACKNOWLEDGEMENT

The author would like to gratefully acknowledge the hours spent by Joseph McMoneagle. He is a peerless individual in the world and will always be understood as an exceptional scientific pioneer into the possibilities of the human mind. I want to thank all the others in the original military unit that I have met, or corresponded with, telephoned, studied under or shook their hands.

I would like to acknowledge the people of the Monroe Institute™ whose pioneering programs help people expand the possibilities of the human mind.

I also want to thank my friends for their patience, support and feedback. And then, to all the wonderful and truly fascinated people, of every persuasion, whose judgment it was that this information be brought forward.

PREFACE

The Joan of Arc case was extremely interesting target to work. Medieval mentalities were completely different than modern thought. What we found out was that Joan did not die by flame and that she was not tied to a wooden stake. The proof of this was hiding in plain sight and is revealed along with the world's only portrait of the maiden.

As for the Evidential Details series at large, many agree these books can affect history for two reasons: findings and methodologies. For the first time, Military Intelligence quality Controlled Remote Viewing capabilities were brought to historical mysteries in what academia refers to as *recent modern* – the exception being the Ötzi the Iceman viewing of 5300 years ago. All of it was to develop the most accurate historical information possible. Time will tell as individuals, with peripheral research, provide anecdotal information or produce a document that suddenly fits.

Others have gone so far as to say these findings unlock more fresh data than any particular PhD candidate's History dissertation this year. And it is for this prospect that the reader is encouraged to look deeper into the ulterior motives for opposition.

For information on the origins of the military's involvement with Remote Viewing, kindly refer to our **Beginnings** section. The **Princess Diana Spencer Introduction** was designed to highlight remote viewing nomenclature, and demonstrate viewer integrity.

For any researcher, it is the guarded realization that you have connected unattainable investigational dots that is the most intellectually stimulating factor in any horizon approach to inquiry. My time documenting those points seem to confirm the viability of Remote Viewing as a tool when used in conjunction with other research sources. What I can say is that I have been involved with the most spectacularly fascinating process of historical inquiry ever. As likely the only author to begin historical research with the mystery's solutions in hand, I came to call the confirmational dots the *Evidential Details*.

Chicago - 2013

Inside the Military Intelligence Program known as Operation Star Gate – a comment on developing the Remote Viewing Protocols

We tried a lot of things. Like I always tell everyone, we "improved" on the Ingo (Swann) method a thousand times in a thousand ways. But our bottom line always had to be accuracy, so we had to keep track of the improvements. Most of those times, the resulting data showed that the end result of our "improvements" was to have the accuracy drop down and down and down. Those things which proved over time to work, we kept.

Ingo will be the first to tell you that what we did and taught to new people coming into the unit wasn't his "pure" method. The minute someone would come back from Ingo's training, we would try to see if there was some way to make what they had learned work better in a military / political / espionage setting. Some things did work, and they are now incorporated into the "military" method which passes for the Ingo Swann method.[1]

E-mail from Leonard Buchanan – 7/29/98
Former Data Base Manager for Operation Star Gate

---

[1] The late Ingo Swann was the original psy-experimenter for the U.S. Intelligence and Security Command (INSCOM) and developed the protocols for remote viewing sessions.

Introduction

To

Remote Viewing

A Review of the terminology,
history and capabilities targeting

The Former Princess of Wales Diana Spencer's 1997 Auto Accident

(For the cover story, refer to the Table of Contents)

"When they (University researchers) *did produce an incredibly accurate response during an experiment, it was in even a moderate sense "unnerving." In a greater sense, it was "earth shattering." As* (Stanford PhD) *Russell* (Targ) *implied, for some it was even "terrifying". In no case, was it ever taken lightly, as it always had a tendency to alter one's perspective towards reality and/or our place within it."*

~ Medal Recipient Joseph W. McMoneagle~

It was the peak of the Twentieth Century's Cold War [1945-1990]. The United States, the old Soviet Union, and the People's Republic of China were striving to find new ways to get an intelligence edge. During the years 1968 to 1972, the United States obtained reports that scientists in the Soviet Union had had some success with a telekinesis program that introduced atrial fibulation into frog hearts causing a heart attack.

Realizing the program could target key military and political leaders, and so driven by a threat assessment, the Central Intelligence Agency funded a Stanford University think tank in Menlo Park, California - the Stanford Re-search Institute (SRI) - to conduct an analysis about what humanity through the ages has pondered.

The doctors were to determine scientifically if psy-functioning could be taught, quantified and directed within written protocols. If so, did this represent a credible threat to the people of the United States? Their highly classified "Black Ops" program lasted from early 1972 until November 1995.

Under the most extensive and stringent experimentation that two PhD's could devise, the SRI, supported by other labs and the Army, developed mankind's first "psychic" protocols. "This led to greater understanding of everything from methods of evaluation, to establishing statistical standards, to how a human brain might be appropriately studied."[i] When their findings were made public, many in the academic community were privately stunned.

Eventually this covert military effort focused on real world data collection. As the years of research, analysis and application moved through the 1970's and 80's, Army brass with wholly personal motives, would attempt to quash the program even when research costs did not impact their budget. "All the funding had been approved on a year-to-year basis, and only then based on how effective the unit was in supporting the tasking agencies. These reviews were made semi-annually at the Senate and House select subcommittee level, where the work results were reviewed within the context in which it was happening."[ii]

Fortunately, for The People, the program was given different code names and moved around various Defense budgets until much of the research and development was completed. What emerged was an incredibly "robust" database - and a process - referred to as Controlled Remote Viewing [CRV].

Much of the work took place within the 902nd United States Army Intelligence Group at Fort Meade, Maryland, whose barracks have been demolished. However, from the fastidiously maintained database emerged statistically advanced practitioners; world class viewers whose RV data was the "best in the business." Among these, one remote viewer was the first in history to be decorated with the Army's Legion of Merit and Meritorious Service Awards (with five Oak Leaf Clusters) for having made key contributions to the Intelligence community. This same individual was tasked to unlock the mysteries in this Evidential Details Book Series.

Obviously, accuracy is the name of the game. As with any horizon application process, purposefully moving the human brain into what is likely the mechanics of a sub-quark quantum entanglement required new terminology. As the CRV process was tested, protocols written and cautiously modified, scientists documented mental hazards to viewer accuracy. These hindrances were cataloged and their characteristics differentiated. Year after year laboratory research determined accurate mental representations could be inhibited in a variety of ways. Some of these mental distracters included:

Physical Inclemency - Knowledge of an expected disruption like a phone call or someone about to arrive during a remote viewing session.

Advanced Visuals - A fleeting thought you cannot get rid of before a session.

Emotional Distracters or Attractors - An image you do or do not want to view regardless of the tasking.

Front Loading - Knowledge of what the target is before the viewing session. If localized, it can be used in targeting a feature within the whole picture, perhaps a house in a meadow in front of a mountain. However, without neutral wording like "The target is man-made" the object is generally rendered unworkable.

Analytic Overlay [AOL] - If a viewer is not informed about the target and not front loaded but still has personal information about it, that knowledge may pollute the information stream rendering the session unworkable. Analytic Overlay can be a problem for any viewer. According to the military's former #1 remote viewer:

Joseph McMoneagle - Analytic overlay - CRV [Controlled Remote Viewing], **as a format or method for learning remote**

viewing, offers a structure within which you can discard or identify specific elements within a session for which you are certain or not certain. Analytic Over-Lay (AOL) being a common label for something that falls within the "uncertain" category. However, when studied (under laboratory conditions), there is evidence that fifty percent of the time, information labeled as AOL actuality, wasn't.

I have observed just as many times, someone being smacked up against the side of the head while attempting CRV because they had strayed from the given format and slipped into AOL. I think that sometimes you may forget that CRV was developed within the hallowed halls of SRI and was taught there for years. I saw very little difference in the AOL pitfalls with CRV and other methodologies. I did see that to some extent it was a highly polished technique, which was more easily transferred through training.

With this quick overview of the subconscious transference of recollections, we turn to the remote viewing of the Princess Diana Spencer's accident in the early morning hours of August 31, 1997. As this researcher found, how one targets is critical to the result. In the fall of 1997, the massive press coverage of Princess Diana's accident and funeral emerged as a very real overlay problem. The Hotel Ritz in Paris, France rather than the crash site was targeted. There had been much less news coverage at the hotel. At the time, this target was less than two months old. No accident report had been completed. An envelope, with a second target envelope inside, had been mailed to Joseph McMoneagle's home with nothing more than the targeting coordinates and a date. A skeptical *Life Magazine* reporter was on hand as an observer to write a story.

Mr. McMoneagle requested I submit a target. The viewing event started at 11:49 am on October 29, 1997. What makes these sessions interesting is that the reader can sense the Intelligence intellect. Having viewed 1200 targets in just the last two years of the military's Operation Star Gate alone, this job would reasonably have been assigned to the only viewer to participate in the program for twenty-three years. What was submitted was:

Target Envelope No. 102997 - (no additional information other than what's sealed within the envelope.)

* * *

As her size nine shoes hit the airport tarmac the former Princess of Wales Diana Spencer, 36, knew she was entitled to an escort by that special branch of the French Interior Ministry charged with guarding visiting dignitaries - the Service de Protection des Hautes Personalities (SPHP). But there would be no need of the service once she left the airport. This was to be a private visit.

Diana was returning from a yachting vacation in the Mediterranean off Northeast Sardinia. She and Emad "Dodi" Al-Fayed, [1955-1997] had been aboard the Fayed family's $27 million dollar (US$43.5m/2018), 195 foot yacht *Jonikal,* with 16 crew members.

At this point, "...in her relationship with Dodi Fayed she was displaying a new facet. In some ways a late developer, she had grown up and was simply having some adult fun."[iii] But the couple had been stalked by high-speed paparazzi boats wherever they went. On their last afternoon, they came ashore at the Cala de Volpe in Sardinia and the, "Paparazzi swarmed around them like bees, flashing away."[iv] Forced back to the boat, "Things came to a head when a scuffle broke out between three paparazzi and several members of the *Jonikal's* crew."[v]

At about the same time, hundreds of miles away, a 73 year-old grandfather, Edward Williams, walked into the police station in Mountain Ash, Mid Glamorgan, Wales. He reported to the police he had had a premonition Princess Diana was going to die. The police log, time stamped 14:12 hours on August 27, 1997, stated:

"He [Williams] *said he was a psychic and predicted that Princess Diana was going to die. In previous years he has predicted that the Pope and Ronald Reagan were going to be the victims of assassination. On both occasions he was proven to be correct. Mr. Williams appeared to be quite normal."*[vi]

Based on his previous record the police passed this report along to the department's Special Branch Investigative Unit.

Fed up with the non-stop press hassle, on Saturday August 30, Dodi and Diana boarded the Fayed's Gulfstream IV jet at Olbia airport in Sardinia and flew north. They arrived at Le Bourget Airport about 10 miles north of Paris, France at 3:20 p.m. Fayed's butler

Rene Delorm recalled, "Unfortunately, we had a welcoming committee of about ten paparazzi waiting for us."[vii] About 600 feet (183 meters) away was a Mercedes and a Range Rover. "We had all seen the paparazzi, so we moved quickly. We wanted to get out of the plane and into the cars as fast as possible. (Body Guard) Trevor (Rees-Jones) was the first out of the jet..."[viii]

The entourage had a police escort from the airport up to France's highway A-1 leading to Paris. But as they entered the expressway, reporter's cars and two man motorcycle teams immediately dogged them. The paparazzi were armed with powerful, maximum strength, flashes to penetrate deep into the car. Philippe Dourneau, 35, was Dodi's chauffeur. But in the Range Rover vehicle there had been a switch. Assistant Chief of Hotel Security Henri Paul was at the wheel. It is unclear why Paul was chauffeuring and not at the Ritz Hotel as acting Security Chief.

Once on the highway, Dodi instructed Dourneau to pick up speed in an attempt to elude photographers. What ensued was a high-speed pursuit with motorcycle cameramen weaving in and out shooting pictures. The motorcycle whirl was so intense Diana reportedly cried out in alarm that someone could get killed.[ix]

"Then a black car sped ahead of us and ducked in front of the Mercedes, braking and making us slow down so the paparazzi on motorcycles could get more pictures. They were risking their lives and ours, just to get a shot of Dodi and Diana riding in a car. *Unbelievable*", exclaimed butler Rene Delorm.[x]

Dodi was not accustomed to this and after their high seas harassment, his patience was running thin. Pursuing for miles, the paparazzi then used phones to notify photographers ahead to form another gauntlet on the next highway segment. The Fayed cars split up in an attempt to divide the photographers. Some pursued Henri Paul as he drove to Dodi's apartment to deliver the luggage.

Finally, the Mercedes made it to Bois de Boulogne on the outskirts of Paris to visit the Fayed's Windsor Villa. They arrived about 3:45 p.m. Then they were off to the Ritz Hotel in downtown Paris at 4:35. Alerted by the cameramen the hotel entrance was packed with photographers which in turn generated curiosity seekers in the general public.

Once inside the hotel, Diana checked into the second floor Imperial Suite and went to have her hair done. She also made some phone calls. After the accident, London's *Daily Mail* correspondent Richard Kay stated that Diana had called him saying she was going to complete her contractual obligations through November and then go into private life.

Another call was made to psychic Rita Rogers whom Diana had been in contact with since 1994. Just three weeks earlier, on August 12, Dodi and Di had visited Rogers for a reading on Dodi. She warned him not to go driving in Paris. *"I saw a tunnel, motorcycles, there was this tremendous sense of speed."*[xi] Uneasy, Rogers reminded Diana about her readout concerning a Parisian tunnel saying, *"...remember what I told Dodi."*[xii]

At seven o'clock, they left the hotel for Dodi's apartment at Rue 1 Arsene-Houssaye arriving at 7:15 p.m. Here the couple found the street so crowded they could not even open the car door. "The paparazzi literally mobbed the couple," said (32 year old former Royal Marine Kes) Wingfield. "They really disturbed and frightened the Princess, even though she was used to this. These paparazzi were shouting, which made them even more frightening. I had to push them back physically.'"[xiii]

From their third floor apartment, butler Rene recalled:

"...I could see they were being mobbed. I heard the shouting, saw the flashes going off and watched a security guard shove one of the photographers. Dodi did his best to shield Diana as Trevor and Kes fought to clear a path to the door...The princess was ashen and trembling, and Dodi was angry as they stalked through the apartment door..."[xiv]

This was the way it was going to be. Rumors were rife about a marriage proposal and some wealthy publishers made it clear big money was available to the photographer that got the "million dollar shot". But no million dollars was ever budgeted.

Later, after things settled down and Dodi had returned from shopping for two rings at the Repossi Jewelry Boutique, Rene recounted, "I met Dodi as he walked through the kitchen doorway, his eyes gleaming with excitement. It was then that he showed me the ring. [Dodi received a US$100,000/month ($159,290/2018) allowance from his father] *'Make sure we have champagne on ice when we come back from dinner,'* he told me urgently. *'I'm going to propose to her tonight!'"*[xv] Elated, he also phoned this news to his cousin Hassan Yassin that evening.[xvi]

Dodi had the Hotel staff book a 9:45 p.m. dinner reservation at the fashionable restaurant Chez Benoit on the Rue Saint Martin. He also phoned the Ritz staff he would not be returning. As a result, Security Chief Henri Paul departed for the weekend at 7:05 p.m.

At 9:30 p.m., Dodi and Diana left the apartment for dinner but could not get through the crowd at the restaurant entrance. It was clear they could not enter a restaurant together. The enormous number of paparazzi forced Dodi to cancel their night out. The Press was controlling his special night with his special lady. A frustrated Dodi decided they should make the four mile drive to the Hotel Ritz where they could dine in France's only "safe" restaurant. But Security Chief Henri Paul had gone for the weekend and the abrupt change left the hotel staff with no time to prepare for their arrival.

When they arrived at the Ritz, another press riot broke out. It took Diana two whole minutes to negotiate the camera gauntlet the 20 feet from the drive-up to the front door turnstile. The security camera time stamped her entrance at 9:53 p.m. Security man Wingfield said:

"I had to protect her physically from the paparazzi, who were coming really too close to her[.] *Their cameras were right next to her face."*[xvii]

Dodi was furious shouting at his employees about no security to shield the 10-second walk from the driveway. Shaken, the press savvy Diana wept in the lobby. Everyone was upset. With the owner's son angry, and the security force embattled, a decision was made to call the Security Chief back to work. Francois Tendil called Henri Paul's cell phone at 9:55 p.m.

Once safely in their room, Dodi called his father Mohammed Al-Fayed at approximately 10:00 p.m. He said the two would announce their engagement the next week when Diana returned from England.[xviii] "Diana always had the children for the last few days before they went back to school at the start of a new term, so that she could get everything ready and make sure they had the right kit."[xix] On Friday, she had called to confirm her boys would meet her at the airport on Sunday morning.

Dinner was ordered from the hotel's Imperial Suite restaurant. Diana's last meal was scrambled eggs with mushrooms and asparagus, then vegetable tempura with fillet of sole. As Di and Dodi were trying to dine normally, Henri Paul shoved his way back into the hotel through the paparazzi.

For this targeting, the Hotel Ritz Building was tasked using the proper date, time, and location coordinates. As Mr. McMoneagle looked at a double blind envelope, he started:

McMoneagle - I find myself standing next to a man who is inside some kind of a public building. He is approximately five feet, ten inches in height, good build, good condition physically. He weighs about 165 pounds, is clean shaven, light brown hair, right handed, 38-40 years of age, and is not British or American; meaning he probably has another language other than English as his native tongue.[2]

Upon his return, Henri Paul waited around the Ritz for about two hours. He allegedly had a couple drinks at the bar. The Ritz security cameras recorded his behavior which would be used for future analysis. As Chief of Security, he was certainly aware of their placement and recording capabilities.

McMoneagle - Building interior - Where he (Paul) is within the building is inside of a very elaborate corridor. It runs the full length of the building and has lots of gilded paint, mirrors, thick carpets, lots of flowers, and is very fancy. The corridor runs straight out to a front entry which is well lit and very busy (even though my sense is that it is very late at night). There is an area off to the right of this corridor which has a lot of dark paneling and dark colors with a long bar or type of counter. So, this may be the reception area of the hotel or something like that.

Where he (Paul) is standing is where the main corridor intersects with a short corridor that runs off at a ninety degree angle to the left. It intersects with some kind of a smaller staff or receiving area; perhaps a back door to the building. It is recessed and that is where his car is parked.

The Etoile Limousine Company manager Jean-Francis Musa, 39, provided six luxury cars to the Ritz Hotel for their exclusive use. This Mercedes was licensed as a Grande Remise auto meaning only a licensed chauffeur was authorized to drive it.

---

[2] Paul was 167 lbs. and he was 41 years old. He had brown hair and was also balding. His native language was French. He spoke fluent English and some German.

Henri Paul did not possess those credentials.

McMoneagle - Driver orientation - I believe that he (Paul) **drives a cab or limo**...**on the side, because I associate him with a car, which is parked outside and he is thinking about this car, or it seems to occupy his thoughts for some reason. He is mostly interested with driving from point A to point B. I believe he is not alone and get a strong feeling of mixed male/female in energy; which either means his passenger will be gay, or consist of two people--a male and a female.**

Limo is not a stretch limo but a short, black and formal kind of car. I get an impression of a Mercedes emblem or some kind of emblem like that, so I'm assuming it is a very expensive car, could be a Mercedes.[3] **It is formal and black with an extended foot space in the back seat. Four doors. It is very heavy and my sense is that it might be equipped for important passengers — e.g., bullet proof glass, armoring, hardened tires, etc.; which leads me to believe that at least one of the passengers** [Trevor Rees-Jones, 29] **might be a body-guard** [but] **this may be Analytic overlay caused by the excessive feelings of security surrounding this vehicle and driver.**

* * *

Information about Henri Paul's mixed motivations have come to light in the years since the accident. Born one of five brothers on July 3, 1956 in the port town of Lorient, France, he had a Bachelors Degree in Mathematics and Science from the Lycee St. Louis and had won several contests for his skill as a classical pianist. He became a pilot in 1976 but was unable to qualify as a jet fighter pilot when he joined the French Air Force in 1979. Paul did however achieve the rank of Lieutenant while assigned to Security in the French Air Force Reserves.

In 1986, Paul helped setup Ritz Security. He went on to become Assistant Director. On the day of the accident, he was carrying 12,560 francs (US $2,280) and his savings account

---

[3] The Mercedes S 280 sedan, valued at about $100,000 (US$146.520/2015) was engineered with eight advanced safety systems. The car had a reinforced chassis and roof. It had energy absorbing front and rear end crumple zones with electronic traction control. It also had an electronic ESP sensing system, which monitored trajectory with wheel speed to sense cornering speeds.

passbook. Where the money came from is unknown, but he was one of only two men in France that had access to the automobile conversations of Dodi and Di. The ability to advise the press of their plans would have been of great value.

Personal adversity. Henry Paul had recently been passed over for promotion a second time by Hotel Ritz management. The first disappointment had come on Jan 1, 1993 when the nod went to colleague Jean Hocquet even though Paul was obviously in position as the number two security man. Now again, effective June 30, 1997, as "Deputy Chief" he became the defacto head of a twenty person security team while Ritz Management searched for another chief. Now vulnerable, Paul had been informed of this exactly one month before the accident.

Post mortem tests stated Paul had consumed two anti-depressants called Fluoxetine and Tiapride before the accident. Fluoxetine is the active ingredient in Prozac and together these drugs are commonly used to fight alcoholism. When alcohol is introduced, the intoxicant effect is multiplied. On September 17, a more sophisticated laboratory's final report was issued. It stated that Henri Paul had been in, *"moderate chronic alcoholism for a minimum of one week."*[xx] Once this became public, the Ritz's attorneys and Mohammed Al-Fayed found themselves on the defensive. An unlicensed employee now appeared criminally negligent in a multiple wrongful death accident while in Hotel Ritz employment. It became the million dollar shot vs. the Al-Fayeds.

The intoxication driving limit in France is 0.50 grams per liter. One lab report stated Henri Paul's blood alcohol level was 1.87 g/l. This is the equivalent drinking time for eight or nine shots of whiskey in what was found to be an empty stomach. A second, private laboratory's more moderate findings were used in the Final Report. The Paris Prosecutor's Office Report stated:

"On this particular point, numerous expert's reports examined following the autopsy on the body of Henri Paul rapidly showed the presence of a level of pure alcohol per litre of blood of between 1.73 and 1.75 grams, which is far superior, in all cases, than the legal level.

Similarly, these analyses revealed as [did] those carried out on samples of the hair and bone marrow of the deceased, that he regularly consumed Prozac and Tiapridal, both medicines which are not recommended for drivers, as they provoke a change in the ability to be vigilant, particularly when they are taken in combination with alcohol."[xxi]

So had Henri Paul been out drinking? It is known he returned to the Ritz two hours and fifty minutes after departing. But no one ever knew where he was when he received the Ritz phone call. Investigations into who had seen Paul failed to provide a single witness. In Paris, in the fall of 1997, there was a real fear of liability for anyone acknowledging Paul had been drinking in their establishment. Nonetheless, the French media reported *someone* saw Paul drinking "aperitifs" between 7:05 and **10:08** p.m. that evening. "Someone" is wide open. But it means that after he got the call to return at **9:55** p.m., he dallied almost another quarter hour before departing which is hard to believe given the tone of the call. Until now, the critical questions have been where was Paul, and what was he doing, before returning to the hotel?

McMoneagle - I think he was in fact sitting in a small restaurant or coffee shop, very near where he lives. Maybe even on the corner near his house. He was alone as far as I can tell. I think he was in fact drinking coffee. I do not think he was depressed, at least not more than usual. Also, regardless of what might be said, I DID NOT get a sense that he was drunk. It is remotely possible that he was taking some kind of a medication but I doubt it.

Coffee! Not drunk! This flew in the face of the formal investigation. We were now privately aware, months before the controversy started, Henri Paul was not drunk.

Henri Paul was a pilot. Research indicated it was impossible to reconcile allegations of alcoholism with Paul's recent physical examination. Unbeknownst to the authorities issuing the report, just two days before the accident, Paul had completed a "rigorous" physical examination to renew his pilot's license. His *Certificat D'Aptitude Physique et Mentale* showed, "No signs of alcoholism."[xxii] A direct medical conflict supporting McMoneagle. Was Paul really fighting alcoholism? Six months after these sessions, the Ritz Hotel security videos further reaffirmed our material.

Behavioral Psychologist Dr. Martin Skinner commented in Fulcrum Productions documentary for ITV. The doctor stated there were no behavioral signs of drunkenness as Henri Paul waited for

Dodi and Diana.

Skinner: *I don't think there is evidence, from the video, that can suggest he looked drunk. The pictures of him walking up and down the corridor are straight and smooth. He is standing very still and there is nothing in his demeanor, from these videos, to suggest that there are any problems with his competence in this situation.*[xxiii]

Next came a statement from Trevor Rees-Jones, the front seat bodyguard sitting next to Paul. About intoxication, he said:

Rees-Jones: *I had no reason to suspect he was drunk. He did not look or sound like he had been drinking. He just seemed his normal self. He was working. He was competent. End of story. I can state quite categorically that he was not a hopeless drunk as some have tried to suggest. I like to think I have enough intelligence to see if the guy was plastered or not – and he wasn't.*[xxiv]

Neither the bodyguards, nor Dodi, or anyone else at the Hotel detected anything unusual in Paul's behavior. But there was more.

Paul's blood was next reported as containing abnormally high carbon monoxide levels – 20% too much. How this happened has never been determined. But doctors agree it is impossible for a forty year old man, with that much poison in his blood stream, not to look and feel sick - too sick for high speed urban driving. When the press advanced the idea car exhaust was the source of Paul's poisoning, Dodi's father, Mohammed Al-Fayed, put the obvious question: *"How did Henri Paul get 20% carbon monoxide in his blood when my son had none?"*[xxv]

The obvious question is how you can get that much CO^2 into someone's blood stream when, due to an instantaneous death there was no breathing, and the engine had stopped.

During his last month Henri Paul had come to know what it was like to assume the Security Chief's responsibilities while the Ritz Hotel interviewed. He must have been concerned an outside hire may not be as accommodating as his previous colleague boss had been. After setting up the Ritz security operation, and with a decade of service, Henri Paul now faced the possibility of being forced out by a new supervisor uneasy about his hotel security experience. Clearly, Ritz management was not taking care of Paul as

Session Sketch

This drawing provides a rare glimpse intelligence level RV artwork. In this exercise, people and not the building were targeted. But, this sketch could be the third floor at the North Korean Embassy in Moscow, Russia, or any building, anywhere, anytime. As a person was the target, the Hotel Ritz Paris first floor was roughed out at midnight on August 31, 1997. Points of interest are:

1) At the top of the page, the words **Big Bldg** appear;

2) The various circles with an **X** inside indicates where people were standing at approximately 12:15 a.m. on August 31, 1997.

3) On the left, the **Main Door** is shown with an **X** representing the doorman. As the hall extends to the right, the various rooms are notated.

4) Toward the bottom is a **Business** area. As you walk from the front door, **"There is an area off to the right of this corridor which has a lot of dark paneling and dark colors with a long bar or type of counter."**

5) At the top is an **Alcove** with two people inside. These individual's backgrounds – conversations – futures – mental states - deaths can be targeted at any time in the future.

6) Where the hallway comes to a junction there is a **Man**. This is Henri Paul as he monitors the activities in both corridors. What were Paul's private thoughts? "**I associate him with a car which is parked outside and he is thinking about this car, or it seems to occupy his thoughts for some reason.**"

7) Behind Henri Paul is the **Laborer Area**. Next to this is the drawing date and time documenting who was where when.

8) The hallway to the **Side Door**, "**...intersects with some kind of a smaller staff or receiving area; perhaps a back door to the building. It is recessed and that is where his car is parked.**" That recessed area is shown.

9) McMoneagle also shows the **Formal Black Limo**'s position by the back door and correctly identified the automobile's color and manufacturer's hood ornament (bottom right).

Joan of Arc

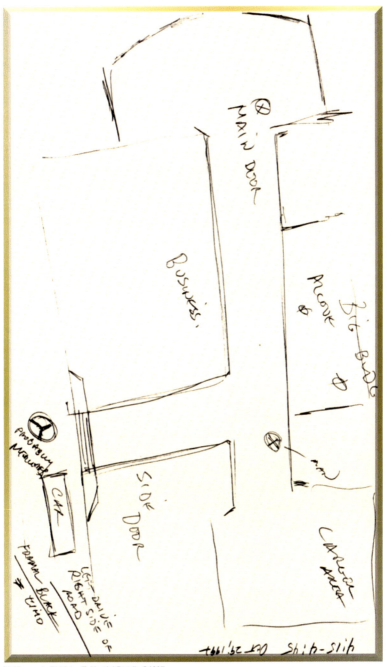

Hotel Ritz Paris first floor with car (lower right) as viewed from Virginia.

a career professional.[4]

Another component of the Henri Paul enigma concerned the fact that most nations have an Embassy in Paris and many dignitaries and diplomats stay at the Ritz. Stories started to appear that Paul was in the employ of various "foreign and domestic" intelligence services. Then it was discovered he had one million francs [US$200,000–$250,000] spread between eighteen bank accounts in an attempt to disguise the fact. Al-Fayed would later make the claim Paul had spent at least three years working for British intelligence. Where he got this information, or if it is true, is unknown. Paul was also allegedly in contact with the Direction General de la Securite Exterieure [DGSE] - French Intelligence. So, we were left with a feigned alcoholic dead man; with employment and big money surveillance concerns; ordered to violate multiple traffic laws; by a romantically aggravated boss in love with the world's foremost beautiful woman.

Henri Paul was uncertain about his future. He had to have been anxious about protecting his access to the Hotel Ritz time and date stamped video-monitoring system. He must have been concerned about his ability to generate good income by documenting high profile business people or foreign dignitary's arrivals and departures.

But all of a sudden, that night there was a positive side to the whole discordant affair. A rare opportunity to make a positive impression on the owner's son was at hand. In the wee hours of August 31, 1997, it would have been impossible for any driver to presume to caution a provoked Dodi Al-Fayed about safe driving on nearly deserted streets. As characterized by French Union Official Claude Luc: "*If one of the Fayeds gives you an order, you follow it. No questions asked.*"[xxvi]

Whatever his prospects, Security Chief Henri Paul was illegally behind the wheel again. He was laid to rest in Lorient, France on September 20, 1997. Father Léon Théraud gave the sermon at Sainte Therese Church.

* * *

---

[4] The Hotel Ritz subsequently hired a former Scotland Yard Chief Superintendent John MacNamara. His background in criminal intelligence management and investigations was substantially different than Paul's Air Force Reserve security credentials.

On Saturday night, now Sunday morning August 31, a physically aggressive horde of stalkarazzi and other onlookers, estimated at approximately 130 people, jockeyed for position at the front door of the Hotel Ritz Paris. Diana Frances Spencer and her boyfriend Dodi, son of Egyptian born multi-millionaire Mohammad Al-Fayed, needed a second car to exit the hotel's back entrance. Because of the paparazzi, a front door - back door scheme had been set-up for their return to Dodi's apartment. Dodi would take Diana out the back leaving his personal Range Rover in front as a decoy.

McMoneagle – Car is parked on the right side of the road (right side driving) which would rule out England, Bahamas, Hong Kong, Japan, etc. It is night and it is dark. The time for this event is current, probably 1985 to 1997. I will try and bring that down to a shorter period later.

The tag on the limo is elongated, with letters and numbers--which is a European style of tag (License 688 LTV 75). **My sense is that there may actually be two colors of tags on this car, or that it has interchangeable tags, which are changed, dependent upon where it is being operated. One is yellow with black lettering; the other is white with black lettering. It may be that there are two different colored tags on the car simul- taneously—one color on one end, one color on the other.**

This is a superb surveillance example. The yellow license with black lettering was on the rear bumper. As it turned out, the color license designated a private car[5]. The white tag is a "for hire" vehicle. From this the reader can gather the type of information available through remote viewing should this car have been driving a foreign dignitary.

After some hallway discussion, Ritz chauffeur's Philippe Dourneau and Jean-Francois Musa drove two decoy vehicles to the hotel's front door. The night was clear. The temperature was 77 degrees [25C]. Their engines were revved up as Dodi and Diana hurried out the back door at 12:20 a.m.

Diana's last few minutes on earth were now inexorably caught-up in the emotional web of her incensed boyfriend and his

---

[5] In Foreign Relations, these plates could indicate a visitor under a territory restriction. If this case, remote viewers could be tasked on who issued both types of plates to the same party. This inquiry would remain secret, while perhaps unmasking a corrupt government official, or a mole inside the host country's bureaucracy.

driver's employment needs. Some paparazzi across the Rue Cabman observed them as Trevor, Diana, and then Dodi came through the turnstile and got into the Mercedes. Henri Paul pulled out and the chase was on.

Associated Press

A back door security camera photograph time stamped 12:19 a.m. just before they departed. It shows Henri Paul (left) conversing with Dodi and Diana with Trevor Rees-Jones head in the background

McMoneagle - Believe the car is the main focus of this target. The man [Paul] may also be of interest.... I believe this target has to do with an accident that probably occurred either in the very late night hours or possibly very early morning hours. Traffic is very light and the streets are very quiet. Get a sense that there are few cars about, in a place which is usually crawling with cars.

The Mercedes is moving very fast from what apparently is a northwest...direction. Have a sense that it goes over an overpass or cloverleaf kind of interchange which then drops straight down into a tunnel.

The car traveled toward the Seine River's west-bound express street referred to as the Cours la Reine. Then they entered the Alexander III & Invalides Tunnel Bridge. The tunnel is 330 meters (361 yards) long.

McMoneagle - It [Mercedes] then exits the tunnel and covers a large curve of open road which enters another tunnel

like area, only this second tunnel is not enclosed completely. Have a sense of concrete tiers on one side... Vehicle is moving very quickly, perhaps in the neighborhood of approximately 100 MPH [162 km/h], maybe even a bit faster (in some spurts or straightaways).[6]

In my opinion, the driver was driving way beyond the speeds that would have been comfortable for the place and time. I believe he was well trained as a driver but not for the place or speed at which he was driving. I have a sense the driver was doing his damnedest to carry out the instructions of those he was carrying, but was operating at speeds and conditions that even he was never really trained to drive within. I think he was the professional here and was being egged on by the passengers.[7]

These sessions took place approximately ninety days before the release of the official fifty-two page report entitled, *Accident de Passage Souterrain de l'Alma. Paris Dimanche 31 Aout 1997, Oh25. Propostition d'Analyse Scientific et Technique. Synthese et Conclusions.* French Engineer Jean Pietri had been commissioned to write an engineering crash analysis, which went on to verify this remote viewing material.

The distance from the first tunnel to the Pont de l'Alma tunnel is 1.2 kilometers (.75 mile). The speed limit is 30 mph (48km). It is here that published accounts differ. Apparently, three people witnessed four to six paparazzi motorcycles attempting to pull alongside the speeding Mercedes. Other accounts say the paparazzi were a quarter of a mile behind when the Mercedes entered the tunnel. In either event, it was all futile. Notified by telephone, reporters had already assembled at Dodi's apartment entrance, million-dollar picture in mind.

McMoneagle – The Mercedes pulls out to pass a slower moving vehicle at a point in the road where the road ahead rises upward to a secondary overpass. Because of the rise in the road, the driver can't see on-coming traffic in time to avoid

---

[6] The curve in the road is 480 meters [.3 miles] in front of the next tunnel, which provides an acceleration area. But with a subsequent curve and dip, it was not possible to negotiate that section of highway at high speed.

[7] McMoneagle was correct on this detail. Paul had attended special driving courses in Stuttgart, Germany from 1988 through 1993, receiving high marks. Dodi knew this.

it, specifically at this speed.

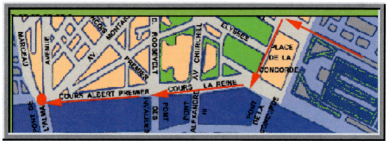

A view of their route along the Seine River. The red arrow
(top right corner) points the direct route to Fayed's apartment.

The final report showed this was correct. French accident investigator Jean Pietri subsequently stated:

"*To our surprise, we observed that the field of view is extremely limited. Passing cars disappear from sight well before they actually enter the tunnel because the descending road is obscured by a retaining wall. To the left the field of vision is blocked by a row of trees.*"[xxvii]

About 40 meters (44 yards) in front of the tunnel the car hit a gap in the pavement, which further destabilized control. As the car passed a white Fiat Uno at break neck speed Henri Paul saw another car dead ahead.

McMoneagle – I believe he sees an on-coming car which appears to be some kind of a black or dark green sedan. I want to say Citreon, but I'm really not sure.[8] Probably a smaller two door car, two passengers; get a sense of dark green or green-black combination, which could mean a green car (body) **and black** (trim).

Mohammad Medjahdi was driving a Citroen BX with girlfriend Souad in the tunnel ahead of the Fiat Uno.

McMoneagle – Dodi's last words - Have a fleeting sense that he [Paul] **is being ordered to go faster and to do more erratic things, to avoid something. He is essentially being ordered to do what he is doing.**

---

[8] McMoneagle was obviously in the car looking through the Mercedes windshield. The use of "oncoming" describes the overtaking of cars. It does not refer to opposite direction traffic flow.

To avoid the on-coming traffic, the Mercedes driver swerves hard to the right and catches the small car he is passing [Fiat Uno] with his rear bumper. Car that was passed was hit. **As a result, the Mercedes slews around left, just misses the on-coming car, which [it] has just passed, and the driver then begins to over-correct his steering.**

Months after these sessions, French engineers confirmed the Mercedes did nick the Fiat Uno and over corrected to the right. Some tail light/head light debris was found.[9] Engineers estimated that if the Mercedes was going 100 miles per hour the debris would have rolled sixteen meters (52.5 feet). That hit took place outside the tunnel and it is here the 18.9m (62ft) tire skid mark begins.

McMoneagle - The Mercedes hits the side to left slews across and hits the right, then swings back to the left, where it catches what appears to be a concrete tier or pier ([#]13 pillar) **of some kind, concrete pilasters, or some kind of upright** (steel reinforced) **concrete dividers, which it hits nearly head on.**

At 12:24 a.m., there was an explosion sound in the tunnel. The subsequent engineering report confirmed Henri Paul's last evasive actions was viewed correctly. Various eyewitnesses recounted the collision. "Gaelle L., 40, a production assistant stated:

"At that moment, in the opposite lane, we saw a large car approaching at high speed. This car swerved to the left, then went back to the right and crashed into the wall with its horn blaring. I should note that in front of this car, there was another, smaller car."[xxviii]

McMoneagle - The Mercedes apparently nearly goes end over end rear to front, but doesn't quite make it [over the top], **instead spinning twice and winds up pointing back in the direction it was coming from.**

The car spinning 1 1/2 times remains unconfirmed. But there was enough inertia for the car to have spun 540 degrees when the rear wheels were off the ground. The impact was so hard that the forward roof area was crushed down to the level of the driver's knees. This is further substantiated by the fact Diana was found

---

[9] The tail light pieces found in the tunnel belonged to a Fiat Uno manufactured between May 1983, and September 1989 by Seima Italiana. The white paint chips were called Bianco Corfu. When found, the car had been repainted.

facing backward in the back seat, which would not have happened with a simple 180-degree turn. N*ewsweek Magazine* reported French police estimated the car had slowed down to 85 mph at the point of impact.[xxix]

The entire trip had taken about four minutes. Trevor Rees-Jones could only recall the Fiat Uno.

Rees-Jones: *"It seems to me there was one white car with a boot which opened at the back* [hatch back]*, and three doors but I don't remember anything else."*[xxx]

He did not leave the hospital until October 4 - thirty-four days later.

Aware Henri Paul did not have alcohol in his system we sought clarification to research about drugs in his blood stream.

McMoneagle - Substance review - I believe if the driver had drugs in his system, whatever kind they were, they were not there by his own hand. I have this sort of strange feeling that he was not deliberately drugged to hurt anyone, but maybe he was drugged to get the car stopped along the route for the "photographers" to get their shots. In other words, his control was tampered with by outside influences. I don't think he was drunk, possibly drugged, but not drunk.

Here the research came full circle. The paparazzi had attempted to slow the Hotel Ritz airport shuttle vehicles earlier that afternoon on the drive from the airport. Once it was discovered, Henri Paul had been an informant for domestic as well as foreign intelligence services we went back to McMoneagle. Could the British government have been involved?

McMoneagle - My sense is that MI-5 (British Intelligence) **did not put the stuff in his drink. However, one might contemplate that if he** [Paul] **was willing to take money from foreign intelligence operatives, he most certainly would have been open to taking money from the Paparazzi. Maybe they were hedging their bets by having a small "drink" with him in the bar before he started driving.**

And what of the high carbon dioxide levels in Dodi's blood stream? Since this viewing, there were reports of a carbon monoxide suicide in Paris that night.

McMoneagle - You have to open your perception a little bit here. He did not have to have any evidence of CO2 in his

blood for them to find CO2 in a blood sample. You only have to switch the samples at the hospital, the morgue, or the lab. Or, pay off the guy who is doing the tests. You could also conceivably rig the test equipment. Also, there are drugs, which will give a false reading as well.

His being drugged enough to cause the accident could be attributed to a drug delivered in coffee, tea, or a drink beforehand. It could also have been sprayed on the inner edge of his door handle (driver's side), painted on the steering wheel, or inside a pair of driving gloves. He could have been shot with a needle delivery system, or pricked his hand, finger, leg, or almost any part of his anatomy on a delivery system getting into or out of the car. It can even be filmed across the pages of a book or map that he might have used to check directions on.

If he had a normal medical condition, they could have used a drug, which reacts violently with the drugs he is already taking for the medical condition. In which case they would either get false readings, or evidence of his medicinal drug, plus some other known drug which would not have been viewed as culprit in the event, simply because no one recognized the possible expected reaction. You also have problems with drugs which are binary in nature and can be delivered in two sittings, so to speak, where the victim gets part A in the morning with breakfast, part B in the evening with dinner, both of which are enzymes and when mixed... cause everything from hallucinogenic behavior, to strokes.

Now we turn to what Dodi and Diana where thinking.

McMoneagle - Back seat travelers - MAJOR PROBLEM: When I try to access others who might have been in the car, I get heavy [analytic] overlay and interference as relates to Diana's death in France. My head fills up with all kinds of motorcycles, and all kinds of news... that was being broadcast about the incident. I believe there were at least two others in this target car, but digging anything out of the overlay is completely impossible.

There is a sense from the people in the back seat that they want to be alone together, but again, I then get overwhelmed with all the Princess Diana stuff... and it all runs together. So, I can't begin to tell where [the] overlay begins and

real data ends. Would prefer to say nothing.

It's rather interesting. I actually have not opened the envelope nor have a clue as to the real target here; but I am being overwhelmed with overlay which is self-generated. Must have been a lot of energy around the Princess Diana stuff. Better to just go no further with it. End of Session.

An abrupt stop, on a then well-known topic, due to analytic overlay. This is a graphic demonstration of the differences between military remote viewers or storefront psychics and hot lines. The media had been saturated with Princess Diana coverage in the period between the accident and this tasking. A psychic hot-liner would have been able to talk and bill without end about what they "saw". One Operation Star Gate military remote viewer commented, "There are many "*psychics*" who have taken this type of gibberish to a finely honed skill."[xxxi] But, when McMoneagle got to the Mercedes back seat, he stopped the session. In intelligence work when you are not sure of your viewing, you must say so. Any elaboration is unethical as in life and death situations, military viewers must stay grounded in the target's realities.

Analytic Overlay [AOL] is terminology within the Controlled Remote Viewing [CRV] protocols developed by Ingo Swann for the U.S. Military Intelligence Community at the Stanford Research Institute as they developed the nomenclature. AOL can generate bad data. So, can anything be done about it?

McMoneagle - Military research - There were a number of experiments which were run to examine whether or not a remote viewer can identify "AOL" while in session. We found that it could be rarely demonstrated. Most viewers are unable to tell (accurately or consistently) when something was AOL or when it wasn't, while in session.

Facts are; Evidence produced within labs suggests that no one methodology is capable of identifying and extinguishing AOL any better than another over the long haul.

There have been significant runs of very low AOL or displays of almost no AOL which have been done by individual remote viewers. So, there are indications that some people might have a talent for producing less AOL than others. But it does not appear to be method driven since it doesn't hold up in testing across all remote viewers using the same method.

So, why should identifying AOL be important??? It is important because, while you are attempting to learn remote viewing (regardless of method), it makes you think about how and why you are "thinking" about something. It is meant to reduce the speed by which you automatically jump to a conclusion. It also supports the structure and keeps one within it (at least until one becomes proficient enough to no longer need it.)

After the impact, eyewitnesses saw a motorcycle 30 to 40 meters behind the Mercedes slow down to observe the accident and then accelerate away from the scene. At 12:26 a.m., the Paris Fire Department - Sapeurs-Pompiers Unit - received a cell phone call from a Gaelle who was in the tunnel. Within one minute another call went out to the "service d'aid medicale urgente" (SAMU) - a civilian emergency medical service.

Inside the wreck, Diana and bodyguard Trevor Rees-Jones were still alive. One eye witness said he heard a woman crying loudly. One of the paparazzi, Romuald Rat, indicated Diana was conscious. He claimed he told her to stay calm; that help was on the way. She remained in the car…

Aftermath

Pandemonium broke out as the Press fought each other to get the new million dollar shot. One photographer leaned into the car to reposition Dodi's corpse for a posed picture. Someone else came with video equipment. Within five minutes, Police Officers Lion Gagliardone plowed through the crowd to the car. The police report stated:

"I observe the occupants in the vehicle are in a very grave state. I immediately repeat the call for aid and request police reinforce-ments, being unable to contain the photographers and aid the wounded."[xxxii]

Officer Dorzee: *"I finally got to the vehicle... The rear passenger* (Diana) *was also alive... She seemed to be in better shape* (than Rees-Jones). *However, blood flowed from her mouth and nose. There was a deep gash on her forehead. She murmured in English, but I didn't understand what she said. Perhaps 'My God!'"*[xxxiii]

Ultimately, six paparazzi were held in connection with the frenzy in the tunnel. They were arrested on suspicion of involuntary homicide and failure to assist persons in danger. Excepting the 24-year-old Romuald Rat, 40 was the average age of those arrested. Twenty film rolls were confiscated providing police with the photographic evidence they needed to confirm each man's activities. Three paparazzi got away.

There are no Miranda rights in France, nor is there a right to call an attorney. French authorities can hold a suspect for forty-eight hours before the prisoner must be formally charged or set free. However, it is certain Henri Paul did not have to be drunk or drugged to have had an accident at that speed.

The former Princess of Wales, Diana Spencer, arrived at the Hospital de la Pitie-Salpetriere at 2:00 a.m. She was pronounced dead at 4:00 a.m. It was then she attempted to contact her son William in Scotland. "William had had a difficult night sleep and had woken many times. That morning he had known, he said, that something awful was going to happen."[xxxiv] When he was told of his mother's death he said, "*I knew something was wrong. I kept waking up all night.*"[xxxv]

At 5:00 p.m. Prince Charles, 48, flew into Villacoublay military airfield outside Paris from Aberdeen, Scotland with Diana's sisters Sarah McCorquodale and Jane Fellows. "Diana's sisters spent most of the flight to Paris in tears. The Prince was controlled but clearly very shaken."[xxxvi] By 5:40 p.m. he was greeted at the hospital by the French President and Mrs. Jacque Chirac (1995-2007). Charles was led into a room with his two ex-sisters-in-laws where Diana lay in a coffin. He asked to be alone with the body for a moment. When he came out his eyes were red. The accident was 368 days after the finalization of their divorce.

Diana's coffin, draped in the Royal Standard's yellow and maroon, was flown home by an honor guard in a British Royal Air Force BAe146 military aircraft to Northolt Air Force Base in England. She was then taken to the Chapel Royal at Saint James Place.

Undertaken by Levertons, her September 6 funeral was the largest in England since the death of former Prime Minister and Nobel Literature Prize winner Winston Churchill [1874-1965]. After the morning funeral, it was reported a million people lined the route as the body was taken from London's Westminster Abby. Different accounts estimated two to three billion people watched the day's events as the car traveled the seventy-five miles to Althorpe House. Late that afternoon her body was laid to rest on a 1,254 sq. meter (13,500sqft) island called The Oval in a lake on the Spencer's ancestral grounds. The four hundred-year-old estate was then partially turned into a tourist attraction.

On September 9, 1997, the week after Diana was buried the Al-Fayed attorney filed civil law suits against the French periodicals *France-Dimanche* and *Paris-Match*. The complaint specified invasion of privacy with willful and wanton reckless endangerment when helicoptering "stalkerazzi" got too close over the Fayed's villa in St. Tropez. But, for the Hotel Ritz, the question became who bears responsibility for the accident? Before 1997 was out, the Fayed, Spencer, Rees-Jones and Paul families had all filed papers to be made civil parties to the investigation. Under French law, this allows them to investigate the case file and participate in any damage awards. And as for the Paparazzi's fate:

"In accordance with articles 175, 176 and 177 of the Code of Penal Procedure; The examining magistrates find that there is no case to answer in the case of the state versus the above named [Photographers]."[xxxvii]

In July of 2004, after the planning, funding and construction were completed, Queen Elizabeth II personally opened the Princess of Wales Memorial Fountain in the southwest corner of London's fashionable Hyde Park.

Then, in April 2008, after a three year investigation costing $7.3 million ($8.3million/2016), a six month long British inquest report was released which included the testimony of 278 witnesses with more than 600 exhibits generating an 832 page report stating:

"Our conclusion is that, on the evidence available at this time, there was no conspiracy to murder any of the occupants of the car," Lord Stevens of Kirkwhelpington, who led the inquiry, told reporters as he presented his findings here. *"This was a tragic accident."*[xxxviii]

In September of 2012, the French magazine *Closer* published paparazzi photos of Diana's eldest son's wife Kate Middleton sunbathing topless while at the Queen's nephew, Lord Linley's French chateau. A publically released statement on behalf of the

Duke and Duchess said: "*The incident is reminiscent of the worst excesses of the press and paparazzi during the life of Diana, Princess of Wales, and all the more upsetting to The Duke and Duchess for being so.*"

And as for the need to use remote viewing protocols:

McMoneagle - Pick whatever method you intend to pursue and stick to it like glue. AOL (Analytic Overlay) **is a fact of life and this will always be so. Those of you who can eventually see your way to controlling your inner-driven or more personalized prejudice while internally processing, will probably improve somewhat in reducing AOLs, but AOLs will never entirely go away.**

CRV (Controlled Remote Viewing) **is a "method" derived from a method the military used while attempting to "train" people to understand both protocol as well as what is going on in a remote viewer's head (such as process-sing or the lack thereof). It was also very specifically designed to "preclude" things from being done out of ignorance (during the RV session) that might impact on/or otherwise prevent the act of successful psychic functioning from taking place; in other words, insure that RV could be replicated and would work more times than not.**

I would add that formal testing in the SRI Lab showed that regardless of technique or method-ology utilized, most viewers were unable to consistently identify AOLs when ask- ed to identify them prior to feedback. I have to say most, because "a couple viewers" were able to do so during signifi- cant runs--but this is inherently talent based and not the general or common rule. I remind you all of what is termed the "AH-HA". If it were not for the Ah-ha's, there would not have been a program. At the end of the road, almost anything is right when you have finally come to understand that it is an inherent part of our nature and then you just simply can do it.

∞

Part II

What you are about to read is the data the Intelligence Community would have received had they tasked this event in the interest of the People of the United States of America.

The worst term of all is "psychic." No stable definition has ever been established for it, and there are great hazards in attempting to utilize a term which has not much in the way of an agreed-upon definition.

Supporters do assume that it refers to extraordinary, non-normal (paranormal) activities of mind. But skeptics assume it refers to illusion, derangement and a variety of non- normal or abnormal clinical psychopathologies."

Remote Viewing - One of the Superpowers of the Human Bio-Mind; Remote Viewing and its Conceptual Nomenclature Problems by Ingo Swann (09Jan96)

"Detachment G's[10] viewers looked at projects ranging from the status of a cement plant in a hostile country to the location of Soviet troops in Cuba. Important North Korean personalities were targeted, as well as underground facilities in Europe, chemical weapons in Afghanistan, the presence of electronic bugs in the new U.S. embassy in Moscow, the activities of a KGB general officer, a missing U.S. helicopter, tunnels under the Korean Demilitarized Zone, and numerous buildings whose purposes were unknown to U.S. Intelligence."

Paul Smith in *Reading the Enemy's Mind*

CRV [Controlled Remote Viewing] is a "method" derived from a method the military used while attempting to "train" people to understand both protocol as well as what is going on in a remote viewer's head. It was also very specifically designed to "preclude" things from being done out of ignorance (during the RV session) that might impact on/or otherwise prevent the act of successful psychic functioning from taking place.

Joseph McMoneagle – e-mail January 8, 1998

---

[10] Det G [Detachment G] was the remote viewing program's code name as it evolved from Operation 'Gondola Wish' to Operation 'Grill Flame'. These were the viewers to make the Army's cut between December 1978 and January 1979. "The Army Chief of Staff for Intelligence, Major General Thompson, officially decreed that the program name, embodied in Det G, would be the focal point for all Army involvement in parapsychology and remote viewing." Op cit. Smith

The

Burning

of

Joan of Arc

Coat of Arms bestowed on the d'Arc Family
by King Charles VII, December 25, 1429

with

Histories Only
Portrait of the Maiden

In the year of our Lord 1348, Medieval Europe was gripped with fear, wasting death, pitiful bereavement and prayer. As the grim reaper's scythe tore through the rest of the century, the Black Death took one third of Europe.

For the Roman Catholic Church it was the time of the Great Schism, while an ongoing war between England and France lasted for over one hundred years (1337-1453). In feudal France, authority had disintegrated as the various Dukedoms were left without an overall functioning state. Seen as a good time to press previously negotiated treaty terms, English King Henry V decided to force the unification of England and France.

During Joan of Arc's life time, the political situation in France was complex. With warring among four factions, it was not a nation as in modern times. Rather, France was a confederation of king-doms with names like Burgundy, Brittany and Normandy. In the North, the British invaded to control the key provinces along the English Channel while the French held the interior. Their disputes revolved around cross channel commercial authorizations; French support for Scottish independence from London; English King Edward III's claim to the French throne through his mother's side of this family;[11] and the desire to unite both countries under English rule to stop what emerged as a 100 year war.

In those days, the word France meant regions centering on Paris. Joan of Arc lived in the town of Domremy in the Duchy of Bar, under the Duc de Lorraine. She lived during the final phase of the Hundred Years War which she helped to end.

We join History 365 years after William the Conqueror (1027? - 1087), Duke of Normandy, had conquered the British Isles in 1066. Through the centuries, Normans had intermarried with Anglo-Saxons and were no longer perceived as French. Now they were invaders from across the English Channel. But politically fragmented, a French national consensus did not exist. There was only sectional political intrigue and violence to determine if the French, British or a regional Lord had the local allegiance.

Theoretically, the French had the military advantage. They had a larger population, a stronger economy, local supply, and a

---

[11] The British did not formally renounce this claim until 1802 with the Treaty of Amiens after which the French fleur-de-lis emblem was removed from English royal arms.

bigger and more respected military. But the army was not in play, as marauding militias' brutally subdued town after town. Then despots moved into vacated regions and established control by torturing and killing anyone that had supported a rival. Towns shifted alliances to protect themselves and some to facilitate their trade with England.

Castles were besieged by up to 30,000 troops. Homage was paid. Resentments and antagonisms matured as Cavalrymen raped, pillaged, stole livestock and destroyed crops. French royalty fought in violent and murderous manner without concern for the law. The French throne intrigued with Scotland to be free of English rule. French and English ships engaged in battle. And so it went in medieval France at an expense neither side could afford.

For this target former Military Intelligence Remote Viewer Joseph McMoneagle was targeted on the Rouen, France market square with the proper time coordinates. The target read: *"Describe in detail the scene as it would be observed or known by those present for the target day."*

McMoneagle - I feel as though I've entered a place of great cruelty. A place where law is what the strong say it is, and the strong are those who hold positions of authority. It is a place where cruelty and creativity brought to the act of cruelty are what generates the degree of fear necessary to keep those, who live in sort of the twilight of the times, in line. It is also a time when morality is being bought and sold, even by those who dispense it, and a place where there seems to be very little division between church and state. It is a time of intense poverty, slavery, savagery, starvation, and hopelessness. It is a very dark place in time and history.

Having said all this, I need to say that I feel there is a specific event, but it is framed with a multitude of events that are all significant. There seems to be a play of sorts which is flowing outward in a linear format that is very complex and interactive. It is almost an impossible (viewing) **difficulty separating out the specifics of one event from their interaction or presence within another event of equal or pressing significance.**

In March of 1413, a pious and stern English King Henry V came to power. As the first successor since the 1399 usurpation of the crown by his father, Henry reasserted his claims to the French

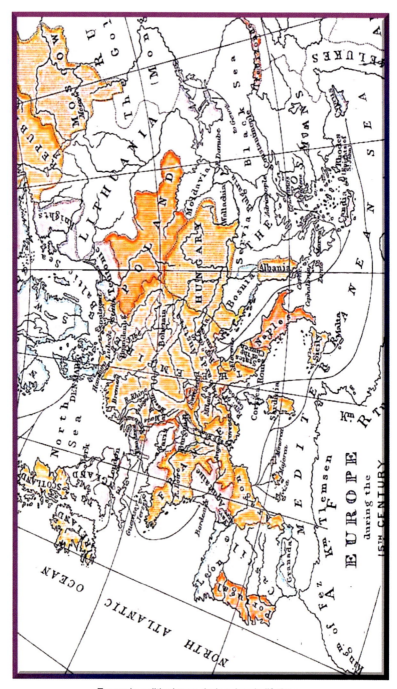

Europe's political map during Joan's lifetime.

throne in hopes of consolidating the two nations, while at the same time uniting England behind his shaky House of Lancaster.

In 1415, the English army boarded warships assembled for the French campaign. Now:

"Suppose that you have seen
The well-appointed King at Hampton Pier,
Embark his royalty: and his brave fleet,
With silken steamers, the young Phoebus (Sun God) *fanning;*
Play with your fancies: and in them behold,
Upon the hempen tackle, ship boys climbing;
Hear the shrill whistle, which doth order give
To sounds confus'd: behold the threaden sails,
Borne with th' invisible and creeping wind,
Draw the huge bottoms through the furrowed sea,
Breasting the lofty surge. O, do but think
You stand upon the (Thames) *rivage, and behold*
A city on th' inconstant billows dancing:
For so appears this fleet majestical,
Holding due course to (Port) *Harfleur. Follow, follow:*
Grapple your minds to sternage of this navy,
And leave your England as dead midnight, still,
For who is he, whose chin is but enrich'd
With one appearing hair, that will not follow
These cull'd (select) *and choice-drawn cavaliers to France?*

William Shakespeare - *Henry V*

English forces captured the port of Harfleur, France on September 23, and moved inland

McMoneagle - I get a sense that this was some time in the past, but not ancient past, nearer to modern than older times, which I'm also trying to iron out. It is difficult to date the (city) **square, but judging by the people who are there, it is pre-gunpowder, or at the very early stages of it. Interestingly, I'm having side effects from this one (or at least empathy effects). I keep getting the worst case of heart-burn whenever I'm targeting it. Interesting huh? Anyway, I have pills for that, so I will continue to march on.**

Looking for a decision, on October 25, 1415, the archers of an English army out-numbered 3 to 1 destroyed the French military at Agincourt in what is considered a watershed event in the military history of the Middle Ages. The French lost three Dukes, seven

Counts, their Commanding General, the Admiral of France, over ninety Lords, and 1,560 Knights.[12] Other French Dukes and Nobles were taken and ransomed. This devastating defeat opened the way

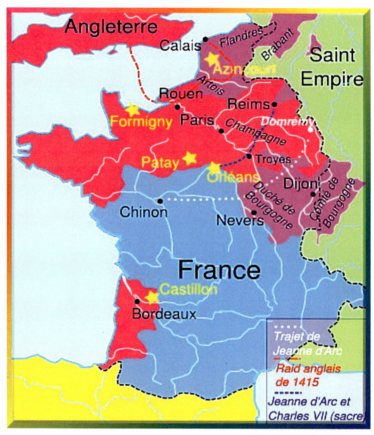

France 1425 - Wikipedia Commons

France in Joan's lifetime. The dotted red line across the English Channel is the path Henry V's army took to the Battle of Agincourt which is a yellow star in Flanders (top middle).The blue area is under French control while the red is under the English. The purple is controlled by the Pro-British Burgundians. Joan's home town of Domremy is shown in white along the green border (upper right). The white dotted line shows Joan's path to Chinon Castle. The Orleans battle is on the road northeast of Chinon (middle). The blue dotted line north from Orleans is the route Joan and Charles took to his coronation in Reims.

---

[12] At Agincourt 8 to 10,000 British defeated 30,000 French using the long bow against armored Calvary. British losses were 500 against 7,000 – 10,000 French casualties. This battle re-established infantry as the main component of late medieval armies, whose use of gunpowder was just beginning to make an appearance on the battlefield but was not militarily decisive until 1450.

for the re-conquest of all of Normandy with a final assault on Paris. But Henry failed to follow-up his victory when he returned to London that November. He left his older brother, John of Lancaster, the Duke of Bedford, as Regent of all English controlled French territory. Joan was just three years old.

English King Henry V (1387-1422) ascended to the throne in 1413 at age 26.

Artist and date unknown - National Portrait Gallery, London

Henry V recognized the importance of control of the sea, and during 1416 is considered to have founded the Royal Navy in preparation for his return to France. By 1417, the psychological impact of the Agincourt losses had Normandy and Burgundy again siding with the British. And the mentally ill French King Charles VI (Charles the Mad) was forced to flee into the interior of France. With no French field army, besieged cities and towns fell quickly. Very few could hold out longer than their food supplies.

During this period the two eldest sons of Mad French King Charles VI died. His son Louis in December, 1415, and son Jean followed in April, 1417. This left the French King's third son Charles as the Dauphin. And so the illegitimate boy that should have never been King was next in succession.

Official portrait of "The Mad" French King Charles VI (1369 -1422) [13]

Bibliotheque National, Paris

In May, 1418 pro-British French forces under John of Burgundy captured Paris. And after a six-month siege, the British entered the city of Rouen in January, 1419. The English seemed unstoppable as Joan turned five years old.

Continued political and military pressure brought the French to the bargaining table. With the capable assistance of Pierre Cauchon, the Treaty of Troyes was signed on May 21, 1420. The terms created a dual monarchy. The agreement allowed the French King and Queen to remain on the throne for the rest of their lives. But the treaty also repudiated the King's son, the Dauphin Charles, as illegitimate hence not eligible for monarchy.

The Dauphin Charles removal from Royal succession was understandable. His mother, Queen Isabella of Bavaria (1404-1463) had apparently had difficulty sleeping with the schizoid King who was 35 years her senior. Between his insane behavior, and concern about bearing a normal child, she likely had extramarital affairs. This was perhaps the reason the King beat her. So the pro-British Isabella signed the throne over to the English and the mad King's

---

[13] Clinical psychologists believe Charles VI suffered from severe schizophrenia whose symptoms first showed themselves in 1392 at age 23, and grew progressively worse. He killed four people at once in a violent rage, would rip up his clothes, was bathed by force, cried in public, hallucinated and told people he carried pieces of iron in his clothing for protection because he was made of glass. He publicly beat and humiliated the Queen.

daughter, Katherine of Valois, went on to plant the family gene of schizophrenia into the British House of Lancaster when she was removed to London.

The French Queen Isabella became the power behind the throne when her "Mad" husband had to be kept from state affairs. She was a pro-English Bavarian who negotiated a Treaty that removed her son Charles from succession. Neither the Queen nor her daughter Katherine supported Charles VII as legitimate.

The treaty also required that Charles youngest daughter Katherine, 18, marry King Henry to consolidate the thrones. That ceremony took place in twelve days at the Church of St. Jean in Troyes, France, on June 2. The dowry was waived as Henry wanted a French son to consolidate England's claim on France. Great Britain now retained treaty control over all occupied French territories. The treaty specified that if Katherine had a male baby by Henry he was to be "Heir of France" and the immediate Regent.

With the Treaty, the British continued their efforts to root out French opposition But during the siege of Meaux, Henry V became ill. He died, probably from dysentery, perhaps poisoning, on August 31, 1422. His legacy to the British Empire was the re-mastery of northern France and establishing its first permanent navy. No British monarch was to travel to France for another 433 years until Queen Victoria in 1855.

Katherine of Valois (1401-1437), daughter of the "Mad King" and half-sister of Charles VII. She was removed to London and crowned Queen. When Henry V died, her son became King Henry VI. Legitimate, she carried the gene of schizophrenia into the British Royal Family that afflicted her son.

Artist Unknown

Eight months before Henry's death a baby boy was born to Katherine on December 6, 1421. But, as a French speaker, she was never considered for English monarchy.[14] Now with his father dead, the new half French – half English King Henry VI ascended to the seat of power for both countries at age nine months.

Just 50 days later, on October 21, the lunatic French King followed Henry V to the grave. And so the year Joan turned ten both the English and French Kings died. Then the officially disenfranchised French Dauphin Charles was betrothed to Marie d' Anjou,

---

[14] An tragic figure, Princess Katherine did not become Queen of England upon Henry's death as he had made no provisions for her. Three years later she may have secretly married Owen Tudor and bore him a son who became father to Henry VII. She died in childbirth at age 36 and was laid to rest in the Westminster's Lady Chapel until her bones were moved in 1668 and again in 1878.

daughter of Duc d'Anjou and Yolande of Aragón. They were married and on October 31, 1422, and a proclamation was issued decreeing the illegitimate Dauphin was now King of France.

The genetically flawed English King Henry VI (1421-1471) Age ten at Joan's death, he too became schizophrenic and was murdered at age 50 probably by the usurper Richard III, Duke of Gloucester.

Artist and date unknown – National Portrait Gallery London

As per the Treaty terms, those cities remaining loyal to the French King were to surrender to the British. But in Central and Southern France the people had not accepted the Treaty. When the French attempted to field a new army, they sustained another devastating defeat at the hands of the Duke of Bedford at Verneuil on August 17, 1424. Joan heard the news as a twelve year old.

On March 6, 1426, Bedford again defeated the French at the battle of St. James, forcing the Duke of Brittany to submit to English authority. Bedford then set about consolidating his control over Northern France.

McMoneagle – John of Lancaster - This is probably a King. I get a sense that he is someone that wears robes of authority and a crown. The crown is more figurative than actual. Like people follow him as the representative of a civil throne (Regent of France). I am having difficulty deciding what throne however, as it apparently is a result of a fusion or mixing of two cultures. There seem to be two

equally matched sides here, which are culturally very different. The throne is also a new one, or one that hasn't existed for a very long period. It is possibly one that's been regenerate as a result of the politics of the time. The King (Regent) thinks he is in charge, but the real power lies with some of the Nobility he has around him, who are connected secretly with the power of the Church.

John of Lancaster, the Duke of Bedford (1389-1435). After Henry V's death, the bagged nosed younger brother became England's Regent of France and Commander of British forces. Completely competent, but with a real fear of witchcraft and hostile because of the military reverses brought on by Joan of Arc, he took a personal interest in making certain her trial ended with a death sentence.

Artist Unknown

As the British proceeded to solidify their hold on France, a demoralized population was caught up in a pillaged countryside whose final political landscape was unresolved. With military reversals, the proclaimed French King Charles became more disposed, as was his personality, to make progress through negotiation rather than war. His primary concerned was maintaining a safe "sovereign" area in central France.

It was during the summer of 1425 that a farm girl from Domremy, France started to hear voices in the family garden. She claimed they were Saints from heaven speaking to her. She kept this to herself but later claimed it was God giving her instructions through the Saints Michael, Katherine and Margaret. Originally, she was very afraid, but they were with her for the rest of her life.

Outside of religion, Joan of Arc's childhood circum-stances are somewhat sketchy. But the medieval living condi-tions of early 15th Century France are fully detailed here in McMoneagle's review of her surroundings in the Rouen town marketplace. Invaluable for students of French medieval archi-tectture, it constitutes an utterly unique and heretofore unavail-able window into the city's condition as observed by Joan on the day of her death.

McMoneagle – City of Rouen - I have a sense there is a major river (Seine), **which runs through this small town, which is the main water supply that is used for drinking, cooking, washing, and even the animals. The drinking water is collected through the use of wagons that haul it in large wooden barrels. This water is collected upstream from the city, and never from downstream. Downstream there appears to be a few mills that use the water to turn large shafts for milling. There are some gutters, but they are only accidental in the way the streets were laid out at a very slight slant to one side or the other, which causes the water to run and collect at some point outside the city when it rains.**

It is a town almost completely built of stone and heavy beams of wood. I also get some structures, which are obviously made from mud, which have been plastered to the outside of what appear to be handmade bricks or cubes of clay. Some of these cubes have been baked - that is, stacked and then having wood put around them and set afire; a primitive and crude way of hardening them. There is a very heavy framework of wood in almost all the structures, but the interior and exterior walls of most are stones that have been set edge-to-edge using a kind of slurry of mortar to seal the cracks. The distance between some of these stones, one from the other is sometimes exces-sive - specifically toward the bottom edges of some of the buildings. Nearly all of these spaces, both narrow and wide are filled with mixtures of dirt, gravel, and whatever else might have happened to be there, which needed to be removed from sight.

Almost all the buildings, regardless of quality, are heated with wood although there are some, which are heated with coal in a very raw form (these could also be chunks of peat

that might look like coal - as my sense is that they are more soft than hard). There is no inside running water anywhere, but there are inside commode facilities in the form of pails -- wooden buckets that must be emptied.

Wood in most of the structures is not refined. It is usually roughly shaped from oak and in very large cross sections. The wood is almost always carved to fit at the ends and kept in place with huge pins of wood. In some cases, there is iron used to wrap the pieces of wood and prevent them from shifting in any way. All exterior walls are buttressed on the larger buildings to keep the heavy stone roofs from causing them to be pushed toward the outside. These buttresses are also chambered or used for crossing from one segment of the larger buildings to the smaller buildings existing within its outer walls.

There are lots of shadows indoors, alleviated with the use of lots of candles at night when it would be particularly difficult to see much, at least within the larger buildings. In the smaller buildings, the people are pretty much limited to a single candle, a small fire in a rough hearth of sorts, and torches dipped in what appears to be tar or pitch for use outside.

The smaller buildings are almost all built of clay, clay brick set in a slurry of clay mixed with straw or horsehair. These brick(s) are laid within a framework of heavy timbers which is all then covered with an outside slurry or mixture of mortar that is made from a special chalk like lime and clay mixture, also mixed with hay or horsehair. The roofs of these smaller buildings are all covered with a thick thatching of reeds or some kind of long grasses that are grown specifically for this purpose. It is as if they used the wheat shafts after the wheat has been taken from them (this could also be barley, or other grain types of stalks.) There are smaller buildings made from stone, but they are not as fancy as the larger buildings, in that their walls are not filled, and they are much colder and damper on the inside as a result. Some of them also have mud floors.

Lighting during the day is very good, except for the interior of some of the stone buildings. The larger buildings also have areas, which are exceptionally dark and shadowy, but there are some rooms with small fires in very large fireplaces made from stone, that take the chill out of the air and provide a bit more light. Most of the rooms in the larger buildings are well lit with light coming in through very large windows. Windows that are filled with what appear to be odd shapes of glass, that are even in the shapes of "lumps" or roughly cut "fragments" in some cases. There is also the use of a lot of iron in the windows of the larger buildings, but very little iron is used in the smaller buildings. The smaller buildings are exceedingly dark and damp, and people who live in them don't seem to be very happy.

With another summer of successful campaigning behind them, English troops moved south into central France. On October 12, 1428, they laid siege to the city of Orleans with its key bridge over the River Loire. After a series of successful military conquests and the political force of treaty politics on their side, the British were taking steps to encircle the French Dauphin. Now supremely confident troops, commanded by the Earl of Salisbury, surrounded the town awaiting the inevitable surrender of slow starvation. But the town held on all winter and the next spring, at the head of a revitalized French Army, an iron maiden appeared on the horizon.

* * *

She has, "more or less disappeared within her legend."[xxxix] Born Jeannette, on January 6(?) 1412, to Jacques Darc and Isabelle Romée de Vouthon in the town of Domremy in the Meuse River Valley she was the fourth child in a family of three boys and two girls. Her parents were Catholic farm folk, "of good repute and decent conversation, according to their condition;"[xl] As a daughter she gardened and helped in the fields at harvest. She took turns guarding the family animals, supported her mother in housework and learned to sew and spin quality yarn. During the week, she would leave to attend church on her own. She was devout and pious in her religious convictions to the extent people would remark upon it. Through court documents, witnesses spoke about her character as, "good, chaste and simple." She was uneducated, possibly rode animals for farm work, but did not come from a warrior family.

What is of interest about this medieval teenager is the dissimilar ways people interpret her. Lost in the mists of time partly because we have no image of her, the whole story seemingly far-fetched. Yet her life was at once splendid, fantastic, ghastly.

How Joan of Arc looked is a modern mystery. If this is her proper proportion on a horse, she was larger than all the men of her day.

Likeness from the Medieval Jean Hordal dissertation frontispiece –1612

There are many volumes written about the Maid of Orleans as she came to be known. Some make her out to be a wonderfully pious saint. But others betray a sarcastic inclination to demean what they call a naïve farm girl who would inevitably die young. There are also attempts to degrade her as illegitimate and even authors that engage in hungry speculation. But many genuine historians have done their best to recount her story accurately.

Through the last six hundred years, what is most available is her court testimony. But as a targeting prospect, it seemed improbable her essence could be grasped in those documents alone. For what continues to haunt detractors is how this farm girl could reverse the high tide of Henry V's military legacy that led to the expulsion of the British from France soon after her death.

In what was then an inconceivable idea, at the age of 17 she told her family she wanted an audience with the French Dauphin. Based on her voices she informed her parents she must go to the town of Vaucouleurs to seek a stranger named Captain Robert de Baudricourt. He was to escort her to the French Dauphin. But when she made the trip to see the Captain he denied her. However, after making three trips between July, 1428 and February, 1429, it was finally decided she would be accompanied by six armed men, on the hazardous eleven day journey, to the Dauphin's castle in Chinon, France.

A Joan of Arc illustration. She never wore a dress. Is this how she wore her hair?

From the Jean Hordal dissertation frontispiece -1612

What kind of a person was Joan? Dame Marguerite La Touroulde, widow of the late Réné de Bouligny, a Councilor to the King testified:

"*I heard from those* (Captain Baudricourt's men) *that brought her to the King that at first they thought she was mad, and intended to put her away in some ditch, but while on the way they felt moved to do everything according to her good pleasure. They were as impatient to present her to the King, as she was to meet him, nor could they resist her wishes.*"

"*Jeanne was very liberal in alms giving, and willingly succored the poor and indigent, saying that she had been sent for their consolation. I have no doubt that she was virgin. According to my knowledge she was quite innocent, unless it be in warfare. She rode on horseback and handled the lance like the best of the knights, and the soldiers marveled.*"[xli]

Eyewitness Catherine, wife of Leroyer, testified at her Nullification Trial:

"Jeanne, when she had left her parents, was brought to our house at Vaucouleurs by Durand Laxart, her uncle; she wished to go to the place where the Dauphin was. I had occasion to know her well; she was an excellent girl, simple, gentle, respectful, well conducted, loving to go to Church."[xlii]

Messire Jean Lefumeux, of Vaucouleurs, Canon of the Chapel of Saint Mary at Vaucouleurs, and Cure of the Parish Church of Ugny testified:

"I know that Jeanne came to Vaucouleurs, and said that she wished to go to the Dauphin. I was then young, and attached to the Chapel of the Blessed Mary at Vaucouleurs. I often saw Jeanne in this Chapel; she behaved with great piety, attended Mass in the morning, and remained a long time in prayer. I have also seen her in the crypt of the Chapel on her knees before the Blessed Mary, her face sometimes bent to the ground, sometimes raised to heaven. She was a good and holy maiden."[xliii]

Sieur De Gaucourt testified:

"*Jeanne*, he adds, *was abstemious* (abstinent) *in food and drink; nothing came from her lips but excellent words, which could serve only for edification and good example. No one could be more chaste... She had always at night a woman in her room. She confessed herself frequently, being often in prayer, hearing Mass every day, and constantly receiving the Sacrament of the Eucharist; she would not suffer any to use in her presence shameful or blasphemous words, and by her speech and actions she showed how much she held such things in horror.*"[xliv]

McMoneagle – It is difficult to tell if this person is a male or female. In some cases, I want to describe this person as a male, in others I want to describe this person as a female. In any event, this person walks a very fine line between both. It is my perception that whether or not this person is male or female is instrumental in understanding the events surrounding them and it will or does have a major impact on the events at hand. This is a significant person, who is important to the numerous events that are all going on simultaneously.

Vigils of Charles VII
Fifteenth Century artwork showing Joan being led to the French Dauphin Charles.

Once at Chinon, she wrote to the Dauphin saying she would know him immediately. So when she was admitted to the castle, Charles disguised himself in a room full of royal courtiers. The Dauphin stayed to the rear of the crowd and was not dressed as royalty. In what was an amazing development, sight unseen Joan wove her way through the crowd and went directly to the Dauphine. This provided a dramatic first impression.

Husson Le Maitre, of Viville, in Bassigny, a Coal Merchant, testified at trial:

"When she came to the King, she recognized him, though she had never seen him before."[xlv]

Feedback: What makes this target so interesting is attempting to understand how she could make herself so powerful in a time when women had no power?

McMoneagle - Perceived power, by those she has contact with. I think in a way, she gets inside their heads and …tells them things she knows which, there is no way she could know unless she has a second sight of some sort. I think she had a way of looking into a person's heart (or soul) in a way

Joan's first audience with Dauphin Charles has been portrayed in different ways. Was she almost bald, or did she have long hair? Both drawings are from the *Vigils of Charles VII.*

Pour la conclusion elure.

Comment la pucelle fit tirer larmee

Drawing of Joan approaching the Dauphine. Was her hair really down to her waist?

that told them she knew exactly what they were thinking. She was probably very psychic in a survival sense of the word. She had a finely tuned sense of knowing what to do at precisely the right time.

I guess a form of RV (Remote Viewing) it could be called. She was able to tell the king things about his life and what was going on in it that no one could have known. I think he believed as a result that she must be speaking for God. This particular king was both a coward, as well as quite a foppish kind of guy[15] -- he was only interested in staying alive and staying out of trouble. I think when he found she could almost read his mind, and his closest advisors saw he believed that, they might have stepped in and used her themselves to get this king to do what he otherwise would not have chosen to do. So, I guess you could say it was a matter of a combination of things -- the nature of the king, the events of the time, and her second sight ability, as well as her being quite naive about being used by the more powerful advisors to the king who had other motivations entirely.

I think she was viewed as very mystical back then, because it was a time of great superstitions. I also think that people were looking for the voice of God in other people. I also believe they were finding and using people like that to enforce the will of the church, local or otherwise. Also, if you lived in the time she did and you met her, you'd walk away thinking this person does not have all her crayons in her box -- a bit over the edge, in a very spooky way. Of course back in these days, it would be viewed as a direct line to God or the Devil which guarantees a good burning either way.

On top of all this, there was a direct intermixing of religion and state affairs; one heavily influencing the other. Priests were Lords and Lords were priests, that sort of thing; lots of torture and killing in the name of God to boot.

Once officially received by Charles, 26, the two spoke at length. She told him her purpose was twofold; 1) to lift the English military siege at Orleans; 2) to have the Dauphin crowned King of

---

[15] Foppish - "A vain, affected man who pays too much attention to his clothes, appearance, etc."- Webster's New World Dictionary, World Publishing. Company.

France in Riems. "It was during this interview, she provided information... that no one knew or could know except God."[xlvi]

A statue of the young Charles VII (1403 – 1461).

Arriving from the farm, Joan looked into the face of this man.

Charles VII tomb sculpture

Amazed, Charles was won over. He authorized her travel to the city of Poitier to undergo scrutiny from clerics, theologians and the faculty of the University of Paris.

But the two weeks of religious scrutiny in Poitier irritated her. When asked to provide a sign she was from God by Brother Seguin De Seguin, Dominican, Professor of Theology and Dean of the Faculty of Theology of Poitiers, he testified he told Joan:

"But God wills that you should not be believed unless there appear some sign to prove that you ought to be believed; and we shall not advise the King to trust in you, and to risk an army on your simple statement.

In God's Name! She replied, *I am not come to Poitiers to show signs: but send me to* (the siege at) *Orleans, where I shall show you the signs by which I am sent."*[xlvii]

McMoneagle – She was God's soldier, fighter, mercen-

ary, whatever you want to look at it. Her prime job in life was to insure that the Holy Roman Church survived and under the appropriate king. She saw her job as cleaning out the heretic and killing off those who would bring dishonor to the Mother Church. She saw herself as one of God's avenging Angels. This was significant back then, as most believed those to be male by nature and not female. She believed just the opposite, from a very matronly belief structure.

Passing the tests, and after a virginity verifying physical examination, the Dauphin ordered a special standard and a full armor suit be made for Joan. The Dauphin also wanted to give her a sword. But in a move that astonished everyone, Joan sent word to the monastery of Saint Katherine-de-Fierbois asking that the monks search for a sword buried beneath the Altar. The stunned monks unearthed a sword and forwarded the weapon to the castle were it was cleaned and decorated.

A very impressed Dauphin now officially sanctioned Joan as a military leader. With French forces in disarray over the last 15 years, a woman who claimed the counsel of God represented hope. Men flocked into this new army swelling the force to between 10 and 12,000 men – a modern division.[16] Her salary was 479 Livres Tournois per year.[17]

To the medieval soldier her army appeared to have a mandate from God, and their unofficial King. And somehow Joan was unusually adept in horsemanship. Pope Pius II wrote:

"The woman was made the leader of war. Arms were brought to her, horses led; the girl mounted with defiance, and burning in her armor, her lance quivering, she compelled her horse to dance, to run, and in no way to turn from its course."[xlviii]

Joan of Arc's battlefield exploits are beyond the scope of this text. There are books written on this part of her life that make excellent reading. The critical component of her victory at Orleans was that, "Her inspirational, if untutored, leadership drove the

---

[16] Some historians have claimed the lowest French troop estimate is 3,000-4,000 soldiers, which would make the odds even longer in her first victory.

[17] The Livre Tournois was the French medieval unit of currency equivalent to one pound of silver. Early Fifteenth Century silver prices are difficult to accurately compute into a 21st century commodity value.

English from their siege lines in defeat, and ended the myth of English invincibility."[xlix] This was done in just ten nights after a siege lasting five months. Her reversal of British military fortunes at Orleans appeared to be something of a miracle. She came to personify God's support for the French cause.

Jean-Jacques Scherrer
Joan leaving the town of Vaucouleurs in February, 1429.

So on March 22, 1429, "Joan the Maid" dictated a letter. The language shows her mind set as she threatened the English Crown and Regent Bedford by name. Her claim to be sent from God unnerved the British. Translated from Old French into Old English, her letter is paraphrased here.

Joan: "*King of England and you, duke of Bedford, you call yourself regent of the kingdom of France ...render your account to the King of Heaven. Surrender to the Maid ...the keys to all of the good cities that you have taken and violated in France.*
     ...I am commander of the armies, and in whatever place I shall meet your French allies, I shall make them leave it, whether they wish to or not; and if they will not obey, I shall have them all killed. If you do not wish to believe this message from God through the Maid, then wherever we find you we strike you there, and make a great uproar greater than any made in France for a thousand years... You, duke of Bedford, the Maid prays you and requests that you cause no more destruction. And give answer... and if indeed you do not do so, be mindful soon of your great damages."[l]

Joan then proceeded to liberate French towns throughout the Loire River Valley culminating in a victory at Patay. At the battle of Jargeau, she was hit in the helmet with a large stone and knocked to the ground while on a scaling ladder. But she told the army to press on and the town was taken.

With these successes, the French military psyche was transformed. The people were now becoming to believe the Maid really had been sent from God - that a live Saint actually led their armed forces. The British too were starting to fear this as a possibility. At the Nullification trial, Simon Baucroix, Squire, testified:

"*In war time, she would not permit any of those in her company to steal anything; nor would she ever eat of food which she knew to be stolen. Once, a Scot told her that he had eaten of a stolen calf: she was very angry, and wanted to strike the Scot for so doing. She was good not only to the French, but also to the enemy. All this I know of a surety, for I was for a long time with her, and many times assisted in arming her.*"[li]

Next Joan wheeled the army north pushing deep into British held territory. She captured Troyes, Chalons and then moved all the way to the city of Reims, east north east of British held Paris. Here she kept her second promise to the Dauphin – that he be officially crowned King of France. Charles, his court and the French Army, entered the evacuated city on Saturday, July 16, 1429. On that Sunday the Dauphine was crowned King Charles VII in direct violation of his parents treaty with the British. Joan was at his side.

Historians agree the lethargic Dauphin would never have undertaken this action on his own.

Is this what Joan looked like?

Jeanne d'Arc Le Brun de Charmettes
(Orléanide - 1817).

But, because of what Joan came to represent, certain members of the French court started to quietly lobby Charles against her for fear of losing some of their own influence. She was a King maker and, "Hence forward Charles and his jealous court did everything in their power to hamper Joan and to restrict her influence."[lii] The King was misled by anti-Joan counselor Georges de la Tremoille toward diplomacy to undercut Joan's operations.

The British were stunned by this summer of reversals. They had lost the initiative and a large amount of territory to a female commander. With the crowning of Charles the VII, their rights to the French throne were officially disputed by a son of the Royal Family. And now towns around the country were starting to turn their allegiance to the new French King even though there was no local French army to protect them.

Now it was the British that petitioned for a cease fire. They wanted "the Maid" dead and 4½ months later, on August 7, 1429, the Duke of Bedford thought her important enough to write Charles VII about turning her over. His letter is paraphrased.

Ladislaus Bakalowwicz 1865
The coronation of Charles VII in the Reims Cathedral with Joan in silver white.

Duke of Bedford: "*We ...make known to you, Charles of Valois, who ...without reason, call yourself King, because you made a new, offensive* (military) *undertaking against the crown ...which build*(s) *a more superstitious and reproved people,* (with) *a disordered and defamed woman, dressed in men's clothing and base in conduct... according to the Holy Scriptures, abominable to God, who by force and power of arms, have occupied... the lands of Champagne and other places certain cities, towns, and castles belonging to my lord the King. ...if you will appear in person with the above-mentioned defamed woman and heretic... we, at the pleasure of Our Lord, will appear on behalf of the lord king in our person. ...and there, if you have anything to offer or place before us, regarding the making of peace, we ...will be inclined and willing in all good ways to make peace...*"[liii]

The dispatch was disregarded and Bedford now took personal control of the English army in France. But it put Joan on notice - if the English caught her she would be treated as a heretic.

Hermann Anton Stilke 1843

Painting entitled *Joan of Arc in Battle*

Joan was confident of ultimate success and focused on Paris. Her army moved the first week in August, 1429. With the new

Simon
Baucroix: "She
would never
permit women
of ill-fame to
follow the army.
None of them
dared to come
into her pre-
sence; but, if
any of them
appeared, she
made them de-
part unless the
soldiers were
willing to marry
them."

A depiction of
Joan in the field
drawn twenty
years after her
death. She
never wore a
skirt.

Martin Le Franc –
1451 - From the
Vigils of Charles VII

French King on the throne, town after town on the road to Paris
surrendered peaceably paying homage to Charles VII's forces. But
unknown to Joan, the Duke of Bedford had reinforced Paris that
same month.

But, with their concern about Joan and the revitalized
French army, Bedford felt compelled to evacuate his entire
government from Paris west to the city of Rouen. And Bishop
Cauchon was now twice uprooted as Joan's forces made him move

Depiction of the difficulties faced by Joan when besieging a castle.

out; once from the city of Beauvais, and again from the city of Riems all the way out of his dioceses.

After an indecisive battle at Montepillory, on the way to Paris, Charles VII decided to "rest" the army in Compiegne. But Joan protested and took the army on a three-day march to the suburbs of Paris arriving during the day of August 26.

Unknown to Joan, Charles VII wanted to slow the army's pace due to his continuing secret dealings with the pro-English Frenchman Philip of Burgundy. Charles hoped to unite the Burgundians with the French against the British, or at least keep them neutral, before he marched on a city like Paris.

Unaware of the politics, Joan's attack on Paris commenced on September 8. At about sunset, Joan took a crossbow arrow in the thigh while in a defensive moat. On the next day, wounded, she sought to renew the attack when she received a summons for an interview with King Charles. She was then angered when the King told her he had decided to hold a council to determine if the attack on Paris was the proper thing to do. It was subsequently determined not to be and Charles ordered the army withdrawn.

Based on his secret agreement, Charles retreated south all the way back to the Loire River basin at Gien and actually dissolved the French army on September 21. This then is how the efforts of the Maiden and her army were brought down. But this secretly negotiated peace was treachery against a naive King. The Burundians simply took the time to regroup against the French Crown. Phillip then renounced the treaty when he was ready, and Charles had to recruit a new army quickly.

With the Paris campaign concluded and her hip healed, Joan was sent to a lesser field of operation against a mercenary named Perrinet Gressart in October of 1429. She was also made subordinate to Lt. General Charles d' Albert. Many in Charles court hoped that she would die in a new army that was woefully under manned and under supplied. And so, after a victory at Saint Pierre-le-Moutier, all offensive activities ground to a halt at the Castle of La Charite-sur-Loire. After a month, the siege was lifted and Joan went to Jargeau on Christmas Day 1429 to find the King had ennobled the d'Arc family with their own coat of arms.

As her force moved north, more men joined up. Her cavalry force of 350 arrived at Compiegne by May 14, 1430. But Joan, who had always taken the offensive, was now on the defensive inside a besieged city. And when the Burgundians realized Joan had arrived, they became intent on taking the town.

Compiegne is situated on the southwestern flowing Oise River which also served as the town's moat on one side. In 1430 there was a gated drawbridge across the river. Between 8 and 9 a.m. Joan led an attack against a Burgundian camp in response to a skirmish that was going on in a meadow across the river

As she prepared to move against the enemy, Georges

Chastellain recounted the scene from his discussion with eyewitness Engurrand de Monstrelet:

"She mounted her horse, armed as would a man, and adorned in a doublet of rich cloth-of-gold over her armor. She rode a gray steed, very handsome and very proud, and displayed herself in the armor and manners that a captain who led a large army would. And in that state, with her standard raised high and blowing in the wind, and accompanied by many noble men, around four hours before midday, she charged out of the town."[liv]

"Philly Statue" honouring Joan of Arc.

She crossed the drawbridge and entered into pursuit of the enemy but it was a trap. As she rode after the retreating soldiers, concealed Burgundian reinforcements, from behind the Monte-de-Claroix Hill, moved to cut off the Compiegne Bridge. Seeing the enemy troops approach, garrison commander Guillaume de Flavy had the drawbridge raised and closed the gate. Questions about treacherous activity and/or pay-offs persist as Joan was now surrounded with no escape.

Giraudon 1880

A depiction of Joan's capture in the Compiegne forest.

After a valiant fight, she was simply overwhelmed by enemy troops who took control of her horse reins. A stout archer rode up from behind, grasped her doublet, and yanked her out of the saddle throwing her to the ground with great force. She surrendered officially to Lionel of Wandomme.

Joan was now a prisoner of the Burgundians and was taken to the castle at Beauevoir. Her imprisonment was not severe as she was able to move around and see people. But she knew the British were bartering for her. And it was while prisoner here she apparently suffered from an inner conflict. In a botched escape attempt she leapt some 60 or 70 feet from the castle donjon.[18] Amazingly, she suffered only a concussion and some bruises. At trial it was alleged that for a woman to have attempted this escape meant she had attempted suicide - a cardinal sin. But the *Chronique des Cordeliers* says she was lowering herself to the ground when her rope broke

After some jockeying between the English and the Burgundians, Jean de Luxembourge was paid six thousand francs ransom raised from a special tax levied on French villages. Joan was handed over to the English on November 21, 1430, and

---

[18] Donjon - "A dungeon; a room in a tower of a castle, often used in early days as a prison." - *Architectural and Building Trades Dictionary,* American Technical Society.

transferred to Pierre Cauchon in Rouen two days later.

McMoneagle - Rouen, France, 1431 - The location for this event is a town of approximately 20,000 people, which should be considered a large town for this particular time in history. I have a sense that it is also a great number of people because of the events currently at hand, especially the prime event. It would also appear to be the beginning event for some things and the ending event for others. It is the culmination of a period of time that, while not very long (Joan's military career) **is very significant to all else that follows** (trial and execution). **In order to get on with it, I intend to break this down into parts that are manageable. There are three major buildings here.**

Fortress Bouvreuil – One apparently is the primary building and occupies a very large area. It is multiple storied and has at least two sub-basements. It is an armored or defensive type of building, much like a castle, only it covers a much larger area.

Church of Notre Dame – To the right side is a section of wall, which also encompasses a second large building that is obviously a church of some kind. It is not particularly large in comparison to some Cathedrals, but it probably would hold more than four hundred people standing comfortably.

Chapel - There is also a (archiepiscopal) **chapel, which is sort of private and exists off to one side, the side facing the larger building. The third large building has two floors and lies across the very large patio or open area. It faces directly into the Church and the larger building.**

As was pre-arranged, the Anglo-Burgundian clergy at the University of Paris called for Joan to be put on trial. Commencing January 9, 1431, it lasted until May 30. The pre-ordained outcome nonetheless needed to appear legitimate. The Judges were a Bishop and a Vicar Inquisitor. There was no voting jury and Joan was not permitted consul until they tried to force one on her near the end in an attempt to gain legitimacy.

McMoneagle - Major Religious Figure - [Pierre Cauchon; (1371–1442)] **- This is probably a Bishop. My inclination was to first say Cardinal because of the power involved, but I get a sense that this was during a period of time when Bishops carried the power of the church. Of course, I am now referring**

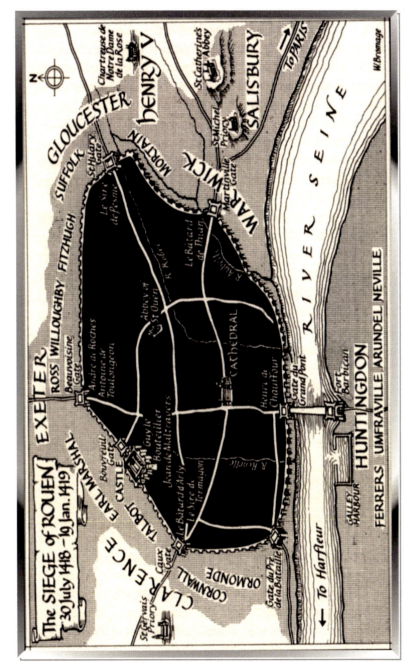

A 1418 Rouen siege map shows the positioning of Henry V's Generals and the buildings McMoneagle viewed. This town is where Joan was executed.

to the Catholic Church. This Bishop has his own agenda and plan, and is using the power of the throne to some extent. He definitely has the ear of the King (Regent Bedford).

Bishop Cauchon was a native of Reims who benefited from the general lack of highly educated clergy at the end of the Bubonic Plague. He was university educated acquiring a Law degree (1398), a Theology degree (1403), and then holding the prestigious position of Rector of the University of Paris, whose allegiance was English.

A diplomat at the General Council of Constance in 1415, Cauchon was acknowledged as a good negotiator on behalf of Henry V's government in the 1420 Treaty of Troyes. His reward was the well-paying appointment as Bishop of Beauvais. He was also paid 1000 Livers per year as an advisor to the English government in Normandy. Now, to be eligible for proper standing in the English court, Cauchon needed to prove he was a worthy prosecutor on behalf of the British occupational government. The upcoming Joan of Arc trial presented itself as a wonderful opportunity to showcase his abilities and commitment.

Thoroughly political, Cauchon was an accomplished jurist and well suited for the task of condemnation. In 1429, he had been forced to flee his dioceses as Joan's army moved north. She now stood before him representing everything he opposed.

Monsieur Jean Lemaitre was the reluctant "Vicar of the Inquisition." He did not like these proceedings, did not show up at Joan's trial until February 20, and not again until March 13. When he was present, he did not participate.

Pierre Cauchon experienced the kind of ethical problems any PhD. would in a rigged capital show trial. First off, by cannon law the accused had a right to be judged by the Bishop in their place of birth or where the alleged heresy was committed. But thanks to Joan, this territory now was under French control. So the Duke of Bedford absolved Cauchon of all jurisdictional difficulties by granting a temporary "commission of territory."

Secondly, even if found innocent, Joan could never be released. This was such a concern that on January 3, 1431, Bedford cautioned the French:

"It is our intention to recover and take back to ourselves that Joan, if so be (it) *that she be not convicted or attained of the case* (of heresy) *or other touching or regarding our faith."*[lv]

This letter was probably accompanied by 765 Livers Tournois. Cauchon acknowledged receipt of that amount on January 31. And several court assessors started to receive 20 sous-Tournois per day. "The intervention of the English in this scene was constant, as it was behind the scenes throughout the trial."[lvi]

McMoneagle - I get a great deal of secretive or manipulative issues surrounding these persons and their involvement with events. There is a deeper plot, a deeper meaning to this mystery than is first evident. I get an impression of a mystery or secret within a secret. A plan within a plan, within a plan; that sort of feeling is predominant to my input.

Behind the scenes this trial was Bedford's, who referred to Joan as, "*a demon in fair human guise.*" The Earl of Warwick was Bedford's trusted go between with Cauchon's office.

The plan within the plan was to condemn Joan of witchcraft and heresy and thereby thoroughly discredit the Coronation of Charles VII as being of the devil. Motivated by the current vacancy of Rouen's Office of Archbishop, Cauchon maneuvered to be appointed Chief Judge at Joan's trial. This affair was also to be a personal payback for Joan's challenging of his ecclesiastical authority. The whole trial was to be upward career mobility for another job well done on behalf of the English Crown.

But in order to achieve the desired outcome, Cauchon was forced to ignore standard canonical rules. He suppressed all positive information and attempted to falsify records. In Joan's postmortem Rehabilitation trial in 1455, a Dominican Brother Isambart de la Pierre, of the convent of Saint Jacques in Rouen, testified about her death sentence:

"*Some of them who took part in the proceedings were pushed into it, like the Bishop of Beauvias, by their partiality. Some others, like the English doctors* (PhD's), *by appetite for vengeance. Others, the doctors of Paris, by lure of gain. Others, again were driven by fear, like the sub-inquisitor and some whom I do not recall; and all this was done on the initiative of the King of England, of the cardinal of Winchester, of the Earl of Warwick and of other English who paid the expenses incurred on account of this trial.*"[lvii]

McMoneagle - The ones with power in this event are the church authorities. They control all with their charges of "heretic." They are using the situation to garner more control

and power over the ruling king or nobles. For some reason they fear the woman they have accused of sorcery. She somehow has power over those she comes into contact with.

Painted by Fouquet, Louvre, Paris
The French King Charles VII – opens the screen for his
official shoulder pads portrait sometime between 1445 and1451.

Joan's courtroom testimony has been kept through the centuries. She is the most documented woman in medieval history. The original Act of Accusations contained 70 clauses which were later revised to twelve. Joan was not permitted to see the written charges. But even though alone in a wholly hostile courtroom without representation, she would not be intimidated.

Joan - to the Court: "*I tell you, consider well ere you call yourself my judge, for you are assuming a great charge, and you charge me too heavily.*"[lviii]

What fascinated the court was her relationship with the Saints. Of this she purposefully refused to be specific.

The Court: "Are you going to speak the truth?

Joan: "*You may well ask me something concerning which I will answer you the truth and to another I shall not answer. If you were well informed about me, you ought to wish that I were out of your hands.*"[lix]

The Court: "Do you know if you are in God's grace?"

Joan: "*If I am not, may God bring me to it; if I am, may God keep me in it. I should be the most grieved woman in all the world it I knew myself not to be in the grace of God...*"[lx]

Because of her piousness, some of her answers were recorded incorrectly and were later ordered corrected. She also seems to have foretold events. In a statement that was in the face of her judges, she declared:

Joan: "*Before seven years be passed, the English will lose a greater gage than they had at Orleans, and they will lose all in France. And the English will suffer a greater loss than they ever had in France and this will be by a great victory which God will send to the French.*"[lxi]

The Pro-English court wanted to suppress this kind of rhetoric.

She was originally accused of erring in her faith and relying on false revelations making her guilty of heresy, blasphemy, idolatry, of promoting religious schism and vaingloriousness. But through the months of trying to prove it, the trial became embarrassingly drawn out and expensive.

As Joan continued to testify, many in the court became aware this was nothing but a political/religious execution intrigue. The evidence simply failed to generate a death sentence and some wondered privately if Cauchon was the right man for the job. When the charge of Witchcraft failed the prosecution was reduced to convicting her of wearing men's clothes and for her apparent refusal to submit to the Church Militant. Failure to yield would render her a heretic. The problem was that the penalty for heresy was not death. She must be brought to the status of relapsed heretic to be burned.

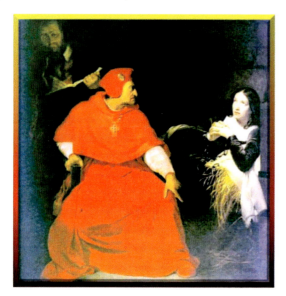

The British Cardinal of Winchester, with transcriber behind, was annoyed with Joan's piousness. Is this what she looked like?

Paul Delaroche - 1824

McMoneagle - There are actually a number of events happening here. One is definitely political and one is religious. But it feels as though the political is using the religious from one side of the event, but the religious is using the political from the other side of the event. I know this sounds complex, but I will attempt to explain it. There is a third event, which is more general and is essentially how the people view things going on. The problem is that most do not understand or are sophisticated enough to know anything about the more sinister or deeper plot aspects of what is going on.

On March 1, 1431, the British annotated their daily payments to the courts assessors. Because of the piousness of Joan's testimony, this trial was beginning to be seen as something that needed to go away quickly and quietly. To officially declare she had died in prison started to look attractive. So in early April there was an attempt to kill Joan with poison fish sent by Cauchon. But it failed and she became very feverish. She was then bled repeatedly and slowly restored to health but the trial had been further delayed and needed, from the British view point, to be stepped up.

On April 2, documentation from the government of Henry VI shows court assessor Beaupere was paid a bonus of 30 Livers-Tournois more than his daily salary for his contributions in the condemnation of Joan. On April 9, British documentation acknowledges payment to all the court assessors of 120 Livers over and above the 240 special allowances they had received for a 40 day period to advance the trial. On April 14, Henry VI's Council authorized payment of 20 Salutes to Jean LeMaistre for his assistance in condemnation. The word had gotten around, condemning Joan paid well.

Then on April 18, Cauchon issued a "charitable admonition" to Joan in her prison cell advising that she was in great danger. Seeing the writing on the wall Joan asked to be buried in holy ground. And sensing the end, on April 21, the English Council authorized another 25 Livers to four top council members.

Joan's second admonition took place on May 2, at which time she said she would submit herself only to the Pope and the Holy Synod in Rome. But her timing could not have been worse.

It is unfortunate that during Joan's lifetime the papacy had been in the turmoil of the Great Schism. In 1415, Pope John XXIII, of the Pisan Line (1410-1415), was deposed in reaction to the findings of the Council of Constance the year before. In 1417 the same council deposed Pope Benedict XIII of the Avignon Line (1394-1423), who nonetheless maintained himself as the true Pope until his death.

Martin V then ascended to the Papacy in Rome (1417-1431). But a challenger, Clement VIII (1423-1429), emerged throughout most of Martin's reign as the "antipope." Outlasting Clement, Martin died on February 20, 1431, during the second month of Joan's trial.

Pope Eugenius IV was then installed on March 3, (1431-1447) but his tenure was marred by political intrigue. Early on, he lost the allegiance of the papal troops and fled to Florence, Italy on May 29 - 48 hours before Joan was to be executed.

Back in Rouen, the prosecution had been stymied with a trial that, due to the pretense of a legal framework, was lasting much longer than anyone expected. Exasperation set in and on May 9, Joan was taken to the Tower of Rouen Castle and threatened with torture. It was demanded she change some of her responses that the prosecution claimed she had, "*answered in a lying fashion*." In what must have been frightening, the tools of torture were displayed and the torturers ready when she replied:

Joan: "*Truly, though you were to have my limbs torn off and send the soul out of my body, I should not say otherwise; and if I did tell you otherwise, I should always thereafter say that you* had *made me speak so by force.*"[lxii]

The torture was put off.

On or about May 13, Joan was propositioned by her original captor, John of Luxembourg, to be ransomed if she would agree never to take up arms against the British again. But it was a trick and Joan saw through it. Regarding a proposed deal she said:

Joan: "*In God's name, you are making game of me, for well I know that you have neither the will nor the power.*"[lxiii]

The ruse had failed and now, due to increasing pressure applied by the Earl of Warwick, 49, events began to quicken. On Wednesday, May 23, Joan was brought before the court and ordered to repudiate her "errors and scandals." She refused. With an English Cardinal and the Bishop of Winchester presiding, the next day she was taken to the cemetery of Saint-Ouen, put up on a burn scaffold, threatened before the public and ordered to renounce her claims.

After a lengthy enunciation by Guillaume Erard[19] it was demanded three times she, "throw herself upon the Holy Church and that she abide by what the clerks and other learned men said and had determined on her sayings and deeds."[lxiv] Whereupon Joan again asked to be taken to the Papal Court in Rome, which was the standard procedure for those formally accused of heresy.

But there was to be no oversight of this trial. After repeated demands on the scaffold, a frightened young Joan "abjured" in front of a crowd on Thursday, May 24. In this abjuration, Joan agreed to

---

[19] On June 8, Erard confirmed the receipt of 31 Livers for the 31 days he had worked on the condemnation of Joan on behalf of the Government of Henry VI.

submit herself to the earthly church and to wear women's clothes. But the seven or eight line text she signed was secretly substituted with a forty-seven line document.

McMoneagle - Events contain many issues of import, which appear to cover a two or three day period, at least in the case of your specific interests. Many elements of some of these events also begin at a much earlier time (start of trial) **…there is a very complex picture here, which hides more than just the specific event of interest** (execution) **and have significant bearing on it. This is especially true regarding a secret that has remained historically hidden for some time. Events of interest are:**

1) A meeting between the Throne (TR) (Regent Bedford) **and the Church Representatives (CR)** (Cauchon)**;**
2) A mock attempt to get the Key Individual (KI) (Joan) **to recant a position relative to the position of the TR and CR;**
3) A mock demonstration before The People (May 24) **in an attempt to deliberately manipulate them;**
4) The Death of KI;
5) The manipulation of events following the death of KI.

Now the expenses ridden British were angered by an abjuration they saw as a way out of the death sentence. As McMoneagle observed a complex picture of political controversy reigned between Cauchon and the British because abjuration meant Joan would now go unconvicted and escape the death penalty. Abjuration only brought a life sentence. Between the infuriated British and the pro-British French, "There was a complete muddle of misunderstandings."[lxv] After all these expenditures, this turn of events put Cauchon under scrutiny.

Taken back to prison, the British were now intent on seeing Joan resumed wearing men's apparel. They intended to apply the verse of Deuteronomy XXII; 5, which originally pertained to cross dressers, homosexuals and female impersonators:

"A woman shall not wear anything that pertains to a man, nor shall a man put on a woman's garment; for whoever does these things is an abomination to the Lord your God."

Joan was now wearing women's clothes shackled in a men's prison with three guards in her cell and two outside. And as could have been predicted, she came under a gang rape attack in the middle of the night. Failing, her attackers took her ripped clothes and threw her a sack of men's clothing. If she put them on, she would be relapsed. But she was left with nothing else to wear. Pro-British jailer Isambart de la Pierre recorded:

"I and several others were present when Joan excused herself for having again put on men's clothes, saying and affirming publicly that the English had had much wrong and violence done to her in prison when she was dressed in woman's clothes. And in fact I saw her tearful, her face covered with tears, disfigured and outraged in such sort that I had pity and compassion on her."[lxvi]

The Bishop was immediately informed. The next day Monday, May 28, Joan was interviewed in prison by Cauchon and others to determine if charges could be brought as a relapsed heretic. She was found wearing a short men's robe with a hood. When questioned she responded:

Joan: *"I would rather make my penitence once and for all, that is to say die, than to suffer any longer the pain of being in prison. I have never done anything against God and against the faith, whatever I may have been made to revoke; and for what was contained in the cedule abjuration, I did not understand it." "If you, my Lords of the Church, had kept and guarded me in your (ecclesiastical) prisons, (it) ...would it not be so with me."[lxvii]*

With this Cauchon left the prison. He said to the Earl of Warwick and a crowd outside, *"Farewell, it is done."[lxviii]*

McMoneagle - I also believe this person is killed or dies as a result of the plots, or segments of the plots to which they have not been made privy. They are essentially used to further the goals of both the Church as well as the Throne (Regent).

The next day forty-two "principal assessors" at her trial were reconvened and Cauchon recounted what had happened in prison. Only three thought she should die the rest believing she should have the cedula re-read to her regarding the gravity of her situation. But under career pressure, that afternoon Cauchon notified everyone Joan was to be taken to the Market Square, denounced as a "relapsed heretic and excommunicate" and handed over to secular justice. It was important to render this long overdue verdict. The wood was ordered.

The next morning Brother Martin Ladvenu was chosen to inform an anxious Joan of her fate. On the morning of the execution, his younger brother Jean Toutmouille accompanied him and recounted what happened:

"And when he announced to the poor woman the death which she must die that day that, so her judges ordained, and understood and heard the hard and cruel death which was almost upon her, she began to cry out grievously and pitiably pulled and tore out her hair."[lxix]

McMoneagle – Rouen Market Square - The location is a small square that is essentially bounded on all four sides by either walls, or outer walls of buildings. There are a couple of common areas, which are generally located alongside or against the very high walls of the larger buildings. These areas are much wider than normal streets and are also finished with cobblestones. These are areas where people gather to talk, or exchange things, as well as general gathering areas. The clearing or open area is approximately 80 meters across, and paved with stone. There is a raised area, or some kind of a platform to one side. It might be a place where things are auctioned or sold. I get a sense that someone stands up on this raised area from time-to-time in front of a crowd of people and hawks stuff.

To the southwest is a row of large buildings that are interconnected (sharing common dividing walls). These buildings are two stories tall with an attic-like space of one large single room used for some sort of storage. These are buildings owned by landlords that is they are constructed for singular purposes of storage and business and are leased or rented. The second floors of these buildings are residential areas also leased or rented.

To the southern portion of this square are stables and smaller buildings grouped around the stables, which also contain some sort of places of business. They are very poor in nature and are only used for specific purposes on special days. Otherwise they are occupied by people and used for residential purposes. I believe these are all one story, with a couple two-story buildings scattered among them. To the east are large

buildings, which are part or portion of a larger estate building or possibly a castle that is also residential in nature. These are also very interconnected, having many apartments as well as having a religious nature about them. They may in fact be shared between religious personages and royalty or at least family of royalty. Basically, this is a major city square used for commerce... It is a marketplace.

Joan gave her last confession to Brother Ladvenu and then requested the Sacrament of the Eucharist. But this presented a problem for a person of official relapsed heretic status. That morning Cauchon consulted with several people on the matter and allowed it. But she was given the sacrament in such disrespectful manner that the lack of proper ceremony displeased the clerics and Brother Martin took over the ceremony.

Depending on which source is accepted, she was taken to the Old Market by the church of Saint Sauveur between 9:00 am and noon, Brothers Martin and Jean at her side. One can imagine what it would have been like to move through those streets. Here McMoneagle provides a description of the scene as Joan bumped along in a cart.

McMoneagle – Much of the roadwork surrounding the larger and more ornate buildings is of stone, which looks like hand-cut cobblestones set with their thicker side standing vertically. They are filled in between with sand that has been taken from the riverbank. Many of the side streets and alley ways that run between the smaller buildings are just dirt and are heavily rutted from wagons being run through them when the ground has been soaked from rain. These smaller alleys are not well traveled.

It is difficult to determine the particular time of the event of interest as it seems to span a period of at least twenty-four hours. In that twenty-four hour period, the weather is dry, cold at night, perhaps somewhere between 45 and 55 degrees (F)... (7–13C). **Things are beginning to change to a warmer daytime, but the nights are still very cold at times.**

The time is approximately 10:00 AM. The weather in this particular area is actually rather nice. It is definitely a place with four seasons. I get a strong feeling that the particular season of targeting is probably in the spring season. I get a sense of

awakening, as though from a long period of winter. There is very little wind, and the sun is shining with very little cloud cover. I have a sense that were it raining, it would have had a major effect on the event or at least the timing of the event.

She moved to a market square filled with English soldiers.

McMoneagle - Most people who are armed are carrying daggers and swords. Blades are approximately 1.25 inches across and about a quarter of an inch thick. The hilts (sword handles) **are somewhat well worked, depending on the person carrying them. Clothing seems to be a mix of western European, predominantly that which would have been found in about the late 1300's.**

I have what appears to be some kind of a square or open area inside a circle of stone buildings and some iron gates off to one side. I think there are lots of people there, but they all have different motivations, which is kind of hard to figure out at the moment (or at least well define.) Some seem to be political, some seem to be religious, but there are dualities in both areas - that is factions within factions, each of which seems to be trying to do something against the other, or in support of the other.

There are crowds of people gathered in the square for a number of reasons. First, the square belongs to the people, as it is a marketplace. Secondly, it is mid-morning and normally a time when the people gather there. Third, there is some sort of event, which is both religious as well as political by nature that is planned for this day in this square.

The overall atmosphere is terrible. I get a great sense of fear and anxiety from most of the people. They are torn between two impossible positions. One appears to relate to theology or religion and the other to the state or government.

A young woman is to be punished for her evil deeds against the church. She will be condemned in front of the public and asked to repent one last time and renounce her ways as a witch or unholy one. ...she will be tied to a pillory and then loads of wood will be stacked against her and she will be burned.

There are a number of very interesting aspects going on here, which I will list as I've perceived them.

1. I get a sense of both English and French, but the only language being spoken here is French. That seems to be a bit confusing. I suspect that it has to do with layering that is too refined for my viewing ability, or there is a distinct mixing of culture.

2. There apparently seems to be two separate forces that hold this or portions of this city (English and Burgundians).

3. Everyone seems to be praying very hard for rain and lots of wetness. Evidently, this has something to do with the funeral pyre. The best that I can tell is that if the wood is dry then it will burn too fast and the death will be agonizing. If the wood is wet, then it burns very slowly and creates a lot of heavy wood smoke which essentially suffocates the person being burned which prevents them from suffering when they are in the flames. Seems a bit morbid, but everyone seems to be praying for very wet wood so that this woman won't suffer.

In a deposition, Free Mason Pierre Cusquel stated:

"That was common repute and more or less all the people murmured that a great wrong and injustice had been done to Joan."[lxx]

4. I believe that no one really wants this woman to die. She is being used as some sort of a pawn to try and draw out some sort of battle. The person who can actually come to her defense (Charles VII) however refuses to do so, as that would put him in an untenable position and subject to having a large segment of his army destroyed. He is safe as long as he remains within his stronghold and they (English) can't get to him.

The woman's protector (Charles VII) wants to come to her aid, but does not, because he sees this as a means of taking her power and using it for himself. He otherwise would essentially have to answer to her for his actions, since somehow her decisions are based not on royal whim but rather on church decree.

There is a very large mixture of both church and state here. While on the surface this appears to be almost entirely church sponsored, it is actually a political murder. They are killing this woman because she is some kind of a political threat to the people involved. Of course, it is very difficult to determine where the politics of the situation begin and end, and where those of the church lie. **This is the reason why she is also not rescued. The element of the church that would rescue her, won't, because in this way they turn her into a victim which they can then use as a reason for destroying the** (British) **element of the church that declared her a heretic. Both apparently see some benefit therein to burning her to death.**

The Charles VII painting hangs in the Louvre, Paris. As the official portrait, it shows the monarch at his best. Considered an embarrassment, he did not reside with the Royal family. Probably threatened, and never certain of his future, the way he encountered growing up was written into his eyes long after he was King. He may have been the son of his uncle which eliminated the mental illness gene. Benevolent, he went on to become known as "Charles the Well Served."

.   Once in the square Joan started to pray. Approximately 800 soldiers were present. During her lengthy lamentations, confessions and requests that all the people pray for her several of the English soldiers wept according to eyewitness Jean Massieu. But their fear of Joan was so great that the English army had delayed a siege of the French city of Louviers until after her death

McMoneagle - Your specific event of interest centers within at least four primary individuals and at least that many minor individuals all of which apparently have different motives, different cultures, and different backgrounds. What they all share is an equal desire for power and prestige. Prestige, in this case being, they all want to be feared by those under them; those under them in turn, being predominantly the general population of the area. They play a part in that they are being manipulated to produce an end result that supports an overall plan.

My perception is that it is a day (afternoon), **which is overcast and not overly warm – in the neighborhood of 60 to 65 degrees Fahrenheit** (15-18C). **The sky is cloudy and visibility is probably around 1500 feet. There is the smell of rain in the air and for some reason this makes people nervous. Also, this is advantageous to people who are the ones in focus.**

I get a sense that there has been a lot made of this execution throughout history, but all for the wrong reasons. This woman is a lot smarter than anyone suspects, except for some of the church officials. These officials understand the degree of power she wields and are intent on eliminating her from the picture. They feel that only they should be the interpreters of God's word and no one else, especially a woman. However, they have to be very careful how they do this as she is revered by the common people as being very special – akin to some form of special priestess.

Nevertheless, the woman does have friends in the church as well who totally believe in her mystical role and who are arranging for her death to be a painless one. In her burning before the people, it will appear that she is untouched by the flames because of the way she has been prepared by priests closest to her. I sense the following has taken place:

1. She has been given a very powerful drug, which mediates the intensity of the heat to the point that she appears to not be feeling it.

2. She has had very wet wood stacked thickly about her, so that when it burns it will create a great deal of smoke which will render her unconscious before the heat and flames actually reach her. Again, so that she will not cry out or demonstrate that she is being burned.

3. There is a group of five who have cut the heart from a pig and plan on inserting this within her remains to show that she was not totally consumed by the fire. This is an attempt to show or demonstrate that this particular element of the church was wrong in burning her. It will cause a further rift between the element of the church that burns her and those who wish her safety.

<u>Feedback Question</u>: "You mentioned, '**These officials understand the degree of power she wields**...'. Yet she was a woman without

any rank or authority. Do you know what effect it had on people?

McMoneagle – She personally has no effect. But her history, reputation would be a better word, is blown way out of proportion to what it actually is and this is what carries sway over the people; especially the people who do not know her. I get a sense that the people back in this time are frightfully ignorant. Therefore, they are easily manipulated by rumor or innuendo.

Feedback Question: "You mention "**Her mystical role**." Can you touch base with her and determine what "made her tick" to instill so much respect for her 'power'.

McMoneagle - What made her tick is her firm belief that she has a direct line to God the Creator and that God will only talk to her. ...in those times, this made her someone to fear as most believed it.

Feedback Question: Did anything happen during the afternoon?

McMoneagle - My sense is that there was a period of nothing happening at all. Everyone (is) essentially staying in their rooms, or hanging about in the central square; mostly people eating and just talking. Officially, I think they were just waiting for the sun to get lower in the sky. Burning someone was dark business and everyone thought it should be done closer to total darkness. I get a sense that the woman (who was burned) was allowed to pray with a priest for a number of hours before her death. I also have a sense that while some ridiculed her, she was pretty much left alone by her guards. She spooked them to some degree. I think they truly thought she was possessed of a spirit that was akin to the dark one and getting close to her risked the loss of their soul or eternal damnation. So... nothing much went on while they waited for darkness to come and the burning time. There appears to be a number of reasons for this:

One, **they had to wait for everyone to show up. Most couldn't do so until after all the chores were done on the farm(s) or at the stall(s);**

Two, **some of the dignitaries had to come from as far away as twenty miles;**

Three, **Noon has a specific significance with regard to religious persecution. I believe the local bishop had to say Mass at High**

Noon (High Mass), and there couldn't be anything done with regard to final resolution until afterward in order to insure he was infallible in his decree;
<u>Four</u>, the fire looks better in the dusk and early evening;
<u>Five</u>, it precluded breaking up the crowd which was easier to control after the hours of darkness;
<u>Six</u>, It made it easier for the devil to take her soul.

Vigils de Charles VII
Almost cartoonish, Joan is tied to a stake as Bedford (right) gives the OK. Painted approximately 40 years after her death, this may be the earliest depiction of her at the stake historians have had to consider.

Being there all afternoon the soldiers became impatient yelling out "Well, priest, do mean us to dine here?"[lxxi] During sentencing, Joan was forced to wear the tall head dress of a Pope called a miter. On it was written, "Heretic, relapsed, apostate, idolater." When the triumphant moment came Cauchon loudly announced the sentence:

"We declare that thou, Joan, commonly called the Maid, art fallen into diverse errors and crimes of schism, idolatry, invocation of devils and numerous others...And thereafter, after abjuration of thine errors, it is evident that thou hast returned to those same errors and to those crimes, your heart having been beguiled by the author of schism and heresy... Wherefore we declare thee relapsed and heretic."[lxxii]

After this final denunciation, the process required that she be turned over to secular judges for a determination of sentence. But even though the Sheriff of Rouen was in attendance, this step was dispensed with. The executioner, Geoffroy Theraeg, was then ordered, "Do thine office"[lxxiii] at which point Joan was borne quickly to the pillar by soldiers followed by priests Massieu, Ladvenu and de la Pierre.

Feedback Question: "You mention a pillar, not a stake. What was the shape of the pillar...? Was wood stacked up against her, around her, under her? How did they burn people back then?

McMoneagle - My sense is that it was a stone pillar, approximately half a foot in diameter (at the top). **It is about twelve feet tall and wider at the base than at the top. It is dark from numerous fires. It sits out on a raised area of stone, which is simply about six feet higher than the surrounding flagstones. I believe the wood is stacked around her three segments deep. It looks like oak, which has been cut and split to approximately 8"x8"x16" in size. She is surrounded by a short wall 2.5 feet high, which is created by cord wood cross- stacked.**

Then there are three rows of split cordwood that are leaned inward toward the wall and placed one on top of the other. These stacks are about twelve inches high and leaned inward at about a 25 degree angle. The upper stack of cord wood is almost lying flat and consists of only three runs of wood. Those underneath consist of at least five runs of wood.

All of the wood is well soaked in water, to create as much smoke as possible. Idea being that the smoke will smother her quickly so that she will go unconscious and then die in the flames without a lot of pain.

Feedback Question: "Could you give a description of the woman victim you viewed. As you see her face, is there anyone whose face is known today that she would resemble?

McMoneagle - I'm not sure about who she would resemble today. Maybe a little bit like a South American Sigourney Weaver -- a bit darker you know, darker hair, darker skin, darker eyes, that sort of thing. But, no way was she very tall. This woman is about five foot three inches, perhaps around 120 pounds. I would not call her beautiful, but she has very intense eyes, dark and intense eyes, somewhat recessed.

I have a sense that she was wearing a peasant kind of

dress, just a roughly woven pullover kind of shift. She also had some form of leather woven belt, which was tied in front. No jewelry and nothing else of an individual nature.

Hermann Anton Stilke 1843
Joan on a wooden platform with authorities in attendance. (center right)

Jules Eugene Lenepveu
Wood bundles being stacked in this 19th century depiction of Joan at the stake

I think she was at first nervous and scared, but by the time they tied her to the pillar, she was probably a lot calmer and ready to accept her fate. I think she asked her friends to insure the wood was very wet, soaked, so that when it burned it would suffocate her before she could feel the flames -- and they complied with that. I think she probably lost her sanity at the last minute, and was displaying a lot of strange behavior just before she was burned. Talking to herself, laughing, maybe saying things that were not very nice to those closest to her -- like "I will speak to God and he will insure that you burn in the fires of hell for what you are doing." That sort of thing.

Feedback Question: "Do you think the wet firewood worked? Did this woman's feet or body burn before she suffocated? Any idea how long from the time of totally uncomfortable to dead?

McMoneagle - Wood probably smoldered and smoked for about twenty minutes before it actually spread and caught well enough to see huge flames that reached her actual body. She was probably unconscious in the first ten minutes. So, there were probably no sounds from her aside from coughing and then she silently burned to death. She might have attempted praying while coughing initially, but it would have been quite silent prayers and probably no one nearby would have heard them.

Feedback Question: "You say she was 'spooky'. She looks stern in the picture. Was this essentially a positive or a negative person? Do you think anyone could carry on a conversation with her, or would she have no time for small talk?

McMoneagle – I think she would talk a great deal with whoever wanted to talk with her, but mostly this didn't occur as she was feared...or revered...would be a better word. I think she mostly had a countenance that was stern, more so than not. I think it exemplified her determination to be who she was and to set an example. I think she was almost a machine when it came to living the way she professed that all should live. In other words she saw herself as setting an example that others should emulate which was almost impossible for most people back then to do. One of the reasons she was probably killed in the end.

The whole affair was obviously political with heavy religious overtures, but this was over her head. I think she saw herself as being a victim of a powerful aristocrat of some kind (Bedford), who just wanted her dead because she threatened him in some way. She really didn't have a deeper under-standing for what was going on. I think in a sense she was used for most of her life and this was the end that others had sort of orchestrated for her. It was necessary for her to die and die

horribly in order for them to be able to put her history (achievements) **to rest so to speak.**

McMoneagle RV Art – Evidential Details ©2001
Joan of Arc's previously undepicted burning pillar designed for repeated use and intimidation. Once she was dead, and her clothes burned away, the fire was pulled back so that all could confirm that Joan of Arc, the woman, was dead.

<u>Feedback Question:</u> "You mentioned these proceedings started at 10 a.m., but then mentioned something about 6 p.m. You also said

the burning took 4 hours before it was approachable which would put that at 10 p.m. I wanted to confirm the sequence of events.

McMoneagle – Proceedings started at around 10 A.M. Burning commenced at around 6:00 PM. Burning finished around 10:00 PM. Everything was probably over by around 11 P.M. During the actual burning of her body, the following facts are true, as best that I can sense or ascertain:

1) It is raining;

2) It is dusk when the pyre is lit (around 6:00 P.M.);

3) It takes approximately four hours for the fire to completely burn to the point that her body can be approached;

4) The woman's body is burned to about 80% destruction. Only some charred bones, teeth, and ash remain;

5) A freshly killed pig's heart is produced by fakery and claimed to be hers. This hoax is carried out by the elements of the church that could have saved her but didn't.

Feedback Question: "Any further sense of the group of five that obtained the pig heart.

McMoneagle - They were religious by nature, probably a cult or associated in some way to a small church in the town or city. I have a sense that they were also rebels fighting against another church or place of worship.

These men were probably four Rouen Bachelors in Theology led by the elderly Bishop of Avranches, whose opinions about getting Rome involved with the trial were subsequently "*left out with malice.*"[lxxiv] Curiously, letters written about the pig's heart incident are missing from the text of the proceedings. These details are not mentioned until Joan's Rehabilitation Trial.

The next year Bishop Avranches was formally accused and imprisoned for having taken part in an effort to liberate Rouen from the British. Two other clerks were threatened with being drowned when they refused to attend these proceedings. One was Jean Lohier, who went on to become the Dean of the Holy See in the Papal Court of Appeals.

The next day Joan's remains were thrown into the Seine River to prevent a grave site shrine.

Feedback Question: "Given her mentality, could this woman ever have worked out as a wife and stay at home mother? Any readout on her attitudes toward men?

History's only sketch of Joan of Arc drawn during her lifetime. It is by Monsieur Clement de Fuquembergue on a page margin in the 1431 parliamentary council register. It has always been suspect because it depicts her in a dress. Until now, it was all that history had and no one knew if it was a drawing of her face or a doodle.

McMoneagle – Great question. HELL NO. She was not a mother by any extent of the word. She was a first rate prize fighter trapped in the body of woman. She didn't hate men but but saw them as weak and unable to do the true will of god. She believed that women were the answer to bettering God's world, but only as avenging Angels. I get a sense that she felt she really understood men, and that she understood they needed someone very strong but with a loving nature to lead them -- carrot and stick -- carrot and stick. There is almost a sexual energy to this in fact. It put her into some sort of reverie...

After the execution, Pierre Cauchon became irritable with what were referred to as "uncomfortable premonitions." He ordered friar Pierre Bosquier imprisoned until the next Easter for saying those in charge of the execution were in error. Then on June 7, Cauchon called in his assessor colleagues and had them reiterate for the record the correctness of the verdict. He tried to slip posthumous words into Joan's mouth for the court record and was only blocked when the notary refused to sign off on it. And two weeks later, on June 12, four of his court assessors acknowledged that a payment of 102 Livers from the government of Henry VI's had been split between them.

Troubled, Cauchon pursued "letters of warranty" from London to the effect the King of England would come to any legal defense arising from these proceedings. But for a Frenchman to pursue liability against the English Crown implied questions existed sufficient for legal action. He then wrote Latin justification letters to top European clergy and royalty confirming that Joan had been officially found to be a relapsed heretic.

<u>Sigmund Freud</u>: *"We know of two sources for feeling of guilt; that arising from the dread of* (spiritual) *authority and the latter one from the dread of the super-ego. ...since the persistence of forbidden wishes* (execution) *cannot be concealed from the super-ego."*[lxxv]

Cauchon attended the crowning celebration of the boy-king Henry VI in France, but his hopes of becoming the Archbishop were dashed. And his ongoing need to convince people about the correctness of Joan's demise seemed suspect. His handling of the trial had taken much longer and was more expensive than the English thought necessary. Focusing on the religious legalities of condemnation with a clothing technicality, Cauchon had failed to pursue Bedford's grand plan of discrediting the Monarchy of Charles VII for having been crowned through the efforts of a condemned heretic. And so for these expensive and strategic failures Cauchon was assigned to the smaller Parrish in the town of Lisieux.

After Joan's death, the English resumed military operations in France for four more years. But the, "Nobles and peasants continued to wage a partisan war against the English despite the apparent indifference and lethargy of Charles VII."[lxxvi] A peace deal was finally signed between France and the pro-British province of Burgundy on September 21, 1435, following the Nevers Conferences. This resulted in the Treaty of Arras. In that same year, the French King Charles VII and Queen Marie had a baby girl. They named her Joan (1435-1482).

The next year, in April of 1436, Paris surrendered after the British garrison was starved out culminating in the end of the 100

McMoneagle RV Art – Evidential Details ©2001

Joan of Arc

Facing death, this is history's only portrait.
The eyeliner is to show that her eyes were slightly recessed.

McMoneagle – This was done on the day of her death. I also believe that back then, people always looked a lot older than they do today for the same number of years. You could probably add ten -- for lack of makeup, stress, and way of life alone.

Years War. This was within the time frame Joan had predicted. However, closer to the English Channel, the Duke of Sommerset did not surrender the city of Rouen until 1449.

Pierre Cauchon died suddenly on December 18, 1442, and was interred in an opulent tomb in Lisieux chapel. And through the period since her death, the French people had lamented over the injustice of Joan's execution so much that King Charles VII held new hearings to review her trial's outcome. In 1456, Joan's Trial of Nullification was concluded. In an interesting look at 15th Century legal prose, their Sentence of Rehabilitation concluded:

We say, pronounce, decree, and declare, the (previous) *said Processes and Sentences full of cozenage,* (deceit through the pretense of friendship) *iniquity, inconsequences, and manifest errors, in fact as well as in law; We say…their execution, and all that followed –* (are) *null, non-existent, without value or effect.*

Nevertheless, in so far as is necessary, and as reason did command us, we break them, (original accusations) *annihilate them, annul them, and declare them void of effect; and we declare that the said Jeanne and her relatives, Plaintiffs in the actual Process, have not, on account of the said Trial, contracted nor incurred any mark or stigma of infamy; we declare them quit and purged of all the consequences of those same Processes; we declare them, in so far as is necessary, entirely purged thereof by this present:*

We ordain that the execution and solemn publication of our present Sentence shall take place immediately in this city, in two different places, to wit,

Today in the Square of Saint Ouen, after a General Procession and a public Sermon:

Tomorrow, at the Old Market-Place, in the same place where the said Jeanne was suffocated *by a cruel and horrible fire, also with a General Preaching and with the placing of a handsome cross for the perpetual memory of the Deceased and for her salvation and that of other deceased persons:*

Done at Rouen in the Archiepiscopal Palace, in the year of our Lord 1456, the 7th day of the month of June.

This was the evidential detail confirming Joan was in fact suffocated. Historically, this item has been overlooked as she is always portrayed as having been burned alive at a wooden stake. Joan of Arc was actually suffocated to death (smoke inhalation) on a concrete pillar and essentially cremated on chains holding her wrists. While this affects nothing, it is hoped this provides a greater insight into the event

Joan was later rehabilitated by Pope Calixtus III. As Cauchon's treachery was exposed in Joan's nullification trial his remains were exhumed by protestors and thrown, "into the common sewer." We could find no pictures of him. Some say his ancestry destroyed all likenesses of him.

Some 464 years after the reversal of her sentence, on May 16, 1920, Joan of Arc was canonized a saint by Pope Benedict XV. The 600th anniversary of her death will be in 2031.And as for those that demean women in combat, "We should not denigrate that legacy; instead, we should study it."[lxxvii]

.

Rip tide from accusers ragged,
The Maiden thrust through time,
Thy pensioner's ghastly thoughts,
Look forward back from thine,
But with their warrants brought,
They cared to know her naught,
Their judgment money begrimed,
And so through the dim pastly
T'was Justice merely pantomimed.

Unknown

Some rise by sin, and some by virtue fall.

Shakespeare in *Measure for Measure*

Bibliography

Claudel, Paul, Cahiers du Rhone; 1942

Clin, Marie Veronique and Pernoud, Regine, Joans Report to Friar Jean Pasuerel in Joan of Arc Her Story; St Martin's Press; 1998

Devries, Kelly, Joan of Arc – A Military Leader; Sutton Publishing; 1999

Duparc, Pierre, La Deliverance d'Orleans et la mission de Jeanne d'Arc in Jeanne d'Arc: Une epoque, un rayonnement; Paris; 1982

DuPuy, R. Ernest and Trevor N., The Encyclopedia of Military History from 3,500 B.C. to the Present, revised edition; Harper & Row Publishers; 1977

Freud, Sigmund, Civilization and its Discontents; Chapter 7

Pernoud, Regine, Joan of Arc - By Herself and Her Witnesses; Stein and Day Publishers; 1962

Quicherat, Jules, Pius II, Commentari verum memorabilium quae temporibus suis contingerunt, IV: 510 Paris

Trial of Condemnation of Joan of Arc 1431; [Proces de condamnation et de rehabilitation de Jeanne d'Arc, dite la Pucelle, Paris 1841-1849

Trial of Rehabilitation of Joan of Arc 1455-6 [Proces de condamnation et de rehabilitation de Jeanne d'Arc, dite la Pucelle, Paris 1841-1849; translated by Jules Quicherat] p. 199; translated from Old French to Latin and subsequently 'authenticated' by notaries. Of five original copies three survive. One in the French Library of National Assembly; two others at the Bibliotheque Nationale.

V. Sackvill-West Nicolson - Saint Joan of Arc; Country Life Press; 1936

Part III

...as a result of my own previous exposure to this (remote viewing) *community I became persuaded that war can almost always be traced to a failure in intelligence, and that therefore the strongest weapon for peace is good intelligence.*

~ H. E. Puthoff, PhD. ~

Founder and First Director (1972-1985)
The Military Intelligence program known as Operation Star Gate

JOSEPH W. MCMONEAGLE
CW2, US Army, Owner/Executive Director of Intuitive Intelligence Applications, Inc.

Mr. McMoneagle has 34 years of professional expertise in research and development, in numerous multi-level technical systems, the paranormal, and the social sciences. Experience includes: experimental protocol design, collection and evaluation of statistical information, prototype design and testing, Automatic Data Processing equipment and technology interface, manage-ment, and data systems analysis for mainframe, mini-mainframe, and desktop computer systems supporting information collection and analysis for intelligence purposes.

He is currently owner and Executive Director of Intuitive Intelligence Applications, Inc., which has provided support to multiple research facilities and corporations with a full range of collection applications using Anomalous Cognition (AC) in the production of original and cutting edge information. He is a full time Research Associate with The Laboratories for Fundamental Research, Cognitive Sciences Laboratory, Palo Alto, California, where he has provided consulting support to research and development in remote viewing for 16+ years. As a consultant to SRI-International and Science Applications International Corporation, Inc. from 1984 through 1995, he participated in protocol design, statistical information collection, R&D evaluations, as well as thousands of remote viewing trials in support of both experimental research as well as active intelligence operations for what is now known as Project (Operation) STARGATE. He is well versed with developmental theory, methods of application, and current training technologies for remote viewing, as currently applied under strict laboratory controls and oversight.

During his career, Mr. McMoneagle has provided professional intelligence and creative/innovative informational support to the Central Intelligence Agency, Defense Intelligence Agency, National Security Agency, Drug Enforcement Agency, Secret Service, Federal Bureau of Investigation, United States Customs, the National Security Council, most major commands within the Department of Defense, and hundreds of other indivi-duals, companies, and corporations. He is the only one who has successfully demonstrated his ability more than two dozen times, by doing a live remote viewing, double-blind and under controls while on-camera for national networks/ labs in four countries.

Mr. McMoneagle has also been responsible for his Military Occupational Specialty at Army Headquarters level, to include control and management of both manned and unmanned sites within the Continental United States, and overseas. He was responsible for all tactical and strategic equipment tasking, including aircraft and vehicles, development of new and current technology, planning, support and maintenance, funding, training, and personnel. He has performed responsibly in international and intra-service negotiations and agreements in support of six national level intelligence agencies, and has acted as a direct consultant to the Commanding General, United States Army Intelligence and Security Command (INSCOM), Washington D.C., as well as the Army Chief of Staff for Intelligence (ACSI), Pentagon. He has earned 28 military decorations and numerous awards…

Interview Statement

Question: *Generally speaking, how much if any "a-prior information" should be given a viewer in operations / applications?*

Joseph_McMoneagle: None. Zero. What you can do if the target requires a response or a description of an individual, you can say, 'Describe the individual at (whatever location)' and the location needs to be hidden (would be a number, for instance). If you were targeting let's say a church, and there was an individual in that church, the church would be coded as say, 'location A1'. It would then say, 'describe individual at location A1'. Under no condition can you give any information that is directly pertinent to the target. There is never any front-loading. The reason for this is because the entire concept of remote viewing is that an individual is forced, has no choice, but to use their psi ability to answer the requirement. Any info that is given in any way or form modifies that response in a way that removes/reduces the probability of accuracy.

Human Use

This a quick but fascinating overview on the formally classified application controversy surrounding the Army's Human Use Policies developed to protect soldiers from experimentation.

"In February 1979, the General Counsel, the Army's top lawyer, declared [the RV Program code named] Grill Flame activities constitute Human Use." The Unit, "… was in the middle of the [authorization] process in March 1979 when the Human Use determination was reversed by the Army Surgeon General's Human Use Subjects Research Review Board. Their decision …trumped the Army General Counsel's ruling…"

"On November 20, the Surgeon General's board changed its mind and decided that Grill Flame did indeed involve Human Use. It took until February 1, 1982 to get final approval from the (Joint Chiefs of Staff) Secretary of the Army to continue operations."[20]

New candidates were then issued a warning by a Major General before being accepted into the black-ops 902nd Intelligence Unit.

"Among other things, they noted that if the candidate joined the project, he would be exposed to psychic phenomena at a level and with a frequency that most people had never experienced before. As a result, he might change in certain ways. Ultimately, no harm should come to him, but he might have a new perspective on himself, his marriage, the universe. In a sense, he might become a new man, and a new husband."

The candidate and his wife were advised to talk, "…this over before they made the final commitment to go to Fort Meade."[21]

---

[20] Smith, Paul H., *Reading the Enemy's Mind – Inside Star Gate, America's Psychic Espionage Program*; Tor Non-fiction, 2005; p. 118

[21] Schnabel, Jim, *Remote Viewers: The Secret History of America's Psychic Spies*; Dell Non-Fiction, 1997, p. 270

A Chinese Encounter

The United States is not the only nation to study and use Remote Viewing. Below is a story allowing enthusiasts and skeptics alike a rare look at an incident inside the Unit during the middle 1980's.

The first time it happened was right after [Major] General Stubblebine had briefed me on the project and said that I would be contacted. The next week I was working mid-shift, and one of the afternoons, I lay down for a nap. In that nap, I had a really shallow and lame dream about something I can't remember now. But at one point, right over the top of that dream there was what appeared to be a semi-translucent visual of three people.

One was a very respectable, businesslike slender man in a suit. A second was a very burly, stocky man, also in a suit, and with a very "Texas farmer" face. The third was an...Oriental girl... (I find it impossible to tell the age of oriental women). She was following along behind the two men and watching.

The men came up to me and talked about something, but I couldn't hear them. The girl was standing behind the two men, listening. The faces were very clear. Clear enough that when the two men actually came to [the INSCOM Base[22] in] Augsburg [Germany] to interview me, I recognized them immediately. I could have picked them out of a crowd on the sidewalk. I didn't think anything of the fact that the girl wasn't with them. It would have been odd to have her on a military trip overseas. I thought she was probably someone in the unit.

Months later, when I got to the unit, she wasn't there. I asked about her and neither the director nor Joe [McMoneagle] (the two men who came to interview me) knew who I was talking about. I figured that it was just an AOL (STRAY CAT)[23] and blew it off.

About a year later, I was doing a practice target. The target was a

---

[22] INSCOM is the abbreviation for the Army's Intelligence and Security Command.

[23] A Stray Cat is a viewer acronym describing the Subconscious Transfer of Recollections, Anxieties, and Yearnings to Consciously Accessible Thought

museum at Arizona State University (I didn't know that - I only had numbers). I was describing things lying in glass topped cases, with the cases up on legs and stands, all arranged around the room for easy access, when I noticed that someone at the target site was looking straight at me, as though she could see me. It startled me, and for probably the only time ever, I wasn't startled OUT of the session, but deeper into it.

I looked back at her, and realized that it was the same girl who had been following the director and Joe in my earlier "dream", back in Augsburg. I looked directly at her, and started to say hello, but then she realized that I could see her, too, and she half turned, and disappeared. That threw me out of the session.

Fortunately, [Captain] Paul Smith was my monitor, and ever the curious one, when I told him what had happened, he said, "Let's follow her and see where she went." Through a series of very impromptu movement commands, we finally located her back at the place where she worked ... the Chinese psychic intelligence effort.

She appeared in some of my sessions after that, but rarely. I tried to find her several times, and a few of them succeeded. Apparently, what they defined as "session" and what we defined as "session" weren't the same. Anyway, over time, we struck up somewhat of a standoffish acquaintance.

About a year after that, I hadn't bumped into her again, so I did a session specifically to find her. She was then in college in a very large city, and evidently out of the government's project altogether. When I found her, she acknowledged my presence, and very strongly desired that we not have further contact. I backed out of the session, and haven't tried again, since. Don't cha love war stories?"

Oct. 1, 1998 e-mail from Leonard Buchanan – Former Operation Star Gate
Database Manager, 902 Military Intelligence Unit at Fort Meade, Maryland
Owner of Problems>Solutions>Innovations, Inc.

For more information, see, *China's Super Psychics* by Paul Dong and Thomas Raffill; Marlowe & Co. New York, 1997

Remote Viewing Protocols

Surrounding the military's RV Session Protocols are the Operational Flow Protocols. The tasking agency was the "Customer" whose identity was strictly withheld to avoid inferences leading to Analytic Overlay. First published here, this process was highly classified for over two decades.

"In actual fact, there was pretty much a different work set-up every time we changed directors in the military unit which was pretty often as projects go. As a result, the "ideal plan" was never adhered to. Many times, we had to sort of switch horse in mid-stream. Anyway, here is the "ideal" workflow:

The **CUSTOMER** (Governmental Agency) comes to the unit director with a tasking.
The **UNIT DIRECTOR** meets with the customer and:
1) makes absolutely certain that the customer knows what CRV is and isn't – what it will and won't do.
2) looks the customer's problem over to see that it is the type of work we are best suited for. If not, he suggests a different solution for them.
If so, he then:
3) gets rid of the customer's "test" questions which only take up time and effort and accomplish nothing.
4) gets rid of the unnecessary questions – just fluff questions which the customer would like to have answered.
5) makes certain the questions asked are questions the customer really wants the answers to. There are LOTS of times when the customer will ask, "Who killed the victim", when the information he really wants is, "Where can we find the evidence that will show who killed the victim?"
6) agrees in writing on a set of basic questions which will be answered, once all the fluff and confusion is gotten out of the way.
7) makes certain that the Customer knows that these questions will be answered, and that other information will be provided, if it is found. However, if it isn't found, then the viewers are only responsible for what is being tasked. Follow-on questions will have to be asked later.
8) explains to the Customer the need for accurate feedback.

9) gets a definite commitment from the Customer that such feedback will be given, on each and every viewer's answer(s) to each and every question.

10) sets a commitment date for providing the answers. This must be a realistic date. Every Customer wants answers right now or yesterday, but the unit director needs to impress on the Customer that there are other customers who also have time limits of now or yesterday, and that reality must figure into the planning, like it or not.

11) provides the final list of questions to the Project Officer, along with any background information about the case gained from the customer.

The **PROJECT OFFICER** studies the background information and tasked questions and:

1) determines the main subject matter for each question.

2) decides the project number and fills out all the preliminary paperwork required for starting a new project.

3) provides the list of subjects to the Data Base Manager. The Data Base Manager looks up each information category in the data base and provides the Project Manager with a separate list of Viewers' names as suggested Viewers for each question.

4) determines which Viewers and Monitors should work on each question.

5) looks at the Viewers' and Monitors' existing schedules and determines the project's time line. He may even do a Pert chart to make scheduling easier.

6) "translates" each question into neutral wording.

7) notifies each Monitor and Viewer of the work schedule change.

8) generates an official tasking sheet to hand to each Monitor.

The **MONITOR** receives the tasking and coordinates from the Project Officer, along with any background information the Project Officer thinks the Monitor should know to help the Viewer better perform a productive session. The Monitor then:

1) makes certain he knows the Viewer's likes and dislikes, quirks, micro-movements, etc. If not, these are either looked up or found out from another Monitor who is more familiar with the Viewer.

2) gets information from the Database Manager about the Viewer's strengths and weaknesses. While this carries the danger of a "self-fulfilling prophecy", the Monitor is hopefully trained enough to use the information for formatting the session, rather than for guiding

and leading the Viewer. If the Monitor is not this well trained, this step is passed up.

3) prepares the session workplace.

4) goes through the session with the Viewer.

5) helps the Viewer write the summary, if necessary.

6) after the paperwork is all done, provides both the Viewer's transcript and his (the Monitor's) session notes to the Analyst.

The **ANALYST** receives the paperwork and:

1) familiarizes himself with all the background knowledge.

2) collects the papers from all Viewer/Monitor pairs.

3) looks into his own notes on each and every Viewer to see work profiles (prone to using imagery, prone to using allegories, etc.). The Database Manager can be of help in this step.

4) performs analysis on the session (see the Analyst's Manual).

5) writes up his reports, critiques, summaries, etc. and provides it to the Report Writer.

The **REPORT WRITER** receives all the information from the Analyst and:

1) familiarizes himself with all the available background information.

2) familiarizes himself with all the Analyst's finding, interpretations and comments.

3) writes the final report (see the Report Writer's Manual)

NOTE!!! This includes taking the finalized answer to each Viewer to make certain that what is being reported is what the Viewer actually meant to say.

4) provides the final report to the Project Officer.

The **PROJECT OFFICER** then:

1) receives the finalized answers to each question after the session has been performed, analyzed and prepared for reporting.

2) gives final approval on the final report.

3) passes the final report to the Unit Director for delivery to the Customer.

The **UNIT DIRECTOR** then:

1) contacts the Customer and sets a date and time to go over the report. Information is not given ad hoc over the phone, nor is an "executive summary" provided.

2) meets with the Customer to provide the report.

3) once again makes certain that the Customer understands the CRV process, strengths and limitations.

4) explains what happened, and how each answer was obtained.

5) points out to the Customer that each question has a "dependability rating" beside it which will tell the Customer what each Viewer's track record is on each specific answer to each type of question. He explains how this "dependability rating" can be used by the Customer as an aid to making decisions from the information provided.

6) sets – in writing – a hard and definite "drop dead" date for feedback.

7) if/when feedback comes in, provides it to the Project Officer who handled the case.

8) if feedback doesn't come in, or is received incorrectly, it is returned to the Customer to either, "dun him" for feedback, or to re-explain how feed-back needs to be provided, formatted, etc.

The **PROJECT OFFICER** then:

1) evaluates each Viewer's response to each question against the feedback.

2) provides an evaluation to each Viewer.

3) provides accurate data to the Database Manager for input into the database.

4) completes all summary paperwork for the project.

5) organizes all related paperwork, checks it for completeness, and prepares it for final storage and filing.

The **DATABASE MANAGER**:

1) inputs all received information into the database.

2) "massages" the database to provide information to those who need it. This includes the Training Officer and all Trainers.

3) maintains quality control on the data going in. "Garbage in – garbage out".

The **TRAINING OFFICER**:

1) schedules training times and facilities.

2) keeps evaluation reports on the Trainers.

The **TRAINER**:

1) accompanies new Viewers through the training process, analyzing their needs and   progress every step of the way (see Trainers Manual).

2) makes and keeps records of the Viewer Student's "natural micro-movements". These will be provided to the Monitors along with a Viewer Student's profile of strengths and weakness.

3) advises management of the Viewer Student's progress and advises as to the student's best possible "training track" for providing the most useful and productive Viewer possible.

Needless to say, this is an overview, and not a complete list of responsibilities and obligations. For example, it doesn't cover what goes on in follow-on tasking, etc.

July 23, 1998 e-mail from: Leonard Buchanan– Former Operational Database Manager at the 902nd Military Intelligence Unit - Fort Meade, Maryland and Owner of Problems> Solutions>Innovations, Inc.

Lead-sealed targeting envelops stored in private safes, ...analysis of dozens of independent scientific studies, hundreds of evaluations, an entire army of scientists and oversight committees focused on providing protection against fraud, and periodic reviews for over a twenty-five-year period cannot seem to persuade those who will always find a reason to doubt the existence of the paranormal.

Joseph McMoneagle - *The Ultimate Time Machine*

.There is also a tendency on the part of almost everyone I've seen running a study to have a successful run and then say, "Hey! That gives me an idea! I'll bet that if we _____, it would go even better!!!" From there on, you're just shooting from the hip.

Professionalism includes getting a clean protocol and sticking to it throughout the whole process, no matter what great idea(s) you get. New ideas and changes should be tested on their own at a different time and in a different study.

Lyn Buchanan - e-mail November 8, 1999

The ease with which viewers can move their minds through time is one of the major strengths of Controlled Remote Viewing. In CRV, no distinction is made between time and space as far as any working conditions are concerned. It is as easy in CRV to move back ten days as it is to move back ten feet.

Lyn Buchanan – *The Seventh Sense*

Beginnings

This details the basis for the original black ops program funding. For readers interested in the data that justified more Congressional spending, this secretive overview of U.S. Military History is recommended.

CIA-Initiated Remote Viewing at Stanford Research Institute

by H. E. Puthoff, Ph.D.[24]
Institute for Advanced Studies at Austin
4030 Braker Lane W., #300
Austin, Texas 78759-5329

Abstract - In July 1995 the CIA declassified, and approved for release, documents revealing its sponsorship in the 1970s of a program at Stanford Research Institute in Menlo Park, CA, to determine whether such phenomena as remote viewing "might have any utility for intelligence collection" [1]. Thus began disclosure to the public of a two-decade-plus involvement of the intelligence community in the investigation of so-called para-psychological or psi phenomena. Presented here by the program's Founder and first Director (1972 - 1985) is the early history of the program, including discussion of some of the first, now declassified, results that drove early interest.

---

[24] Harold Puthoff received his BS and MS Degrees in Electrical Engineering at the University of Florida and a PhD from Stanford University in 1967. He went on to work at the National Security Agency at Fort Meade, Maryland as an Army engineer studying, lasers, high-speed computers, and fiber optics. He is the inventor of the tunable infra-red laser. He spent three years as a naval officer and worked eight years in the Microwave Laboratory at Stanford. Puthoff has over 31 technical papers published on such topics as electron-beam devices, lasers and quantum zero-point-energy effects. He reportedly has patents issued in the areas of energy fields, laser, and communications. [author]

Joan of Arc

Introduction

On April 17, 1995, President Clinton issued Executive Order Nr. 1995-4-17, entitled Classified National Security Information. Although in one sense the order simply reaffirmed much of what has been long-standing policy, in another sense there was a clear shift toward more openness. In the opening paragraph, for example, we read: "In recent years, however, dramatic changes have altered, although not eliminated, the national security threats that we confront. These changes provide a greater opportunity to emphasize our commitment to open Government." In the Classification Standards section of the Order this commitment is operationalized by phrases such as "If there is significant doubt about the need to classify information, it shall not be classified." Later in the document, in reference to information that requires continued protection, there even appears the remarkable phrase "In some exceptional cases, however, the need to protect such information may be outweighed by the public interest in disclosure of the information, and in these cases the information should be declassified."

A major fallout of this reframing of attitude toward classification is that there is enormous pressure on those charged with maintaining security to work hard at being responsive to reasonable requests for disclosure. One of the results is that FOIA (Freedom of Information Act) requests that have languished for months to years are suddenly being acted upon.[1]

One outcome of this change in policy is the government's recent admission of its two-decade-plus involvement in funding highly-classified, special access programs in remote viewing (RV) and related psi phenomena, first at Stanford Research Institute (SRI) and then at Science Applications International Corporation (SAIC), both in Menlo Park, CA, supplemented by various in-house government programs. Although almost all of the documentation remains yet classified, in July 1995 270 pages of SRI reports were declassified and released by the CIA, the program's first sponsor [2]. Thus, although through the years columns by Jack Anderson and others had claimed leaks of "psychic spy" programs with such exotic names as Grill Flame, Center Lane, Sunstreak and Star Gate, CIA's release of the SRI reports constitutes the first documented public admission of significant intelligence community involvement in the psi area.

As a consequence of the above, although I had founded the program in early 1972, and had acted as its Director until I left in 1985 to head up the Institute for Advanced Studies at Austin (at which point my colleague Ed May assumed responsibility as Director), it was not until 1995 that I found myself for the first time able to utter in a single sentence the connected acronyms CIA/SRI/RV. In this report I discuss the genesis of the program, report on some of the early, now declassified, results that drove early interest, and outline the general direction the program took as it expanded into a multi-year, multi-site, multi-million-dollar effort to determine whether such phenomena as remote viewing "might have any utility for intelligence collection" [1].

Beginnings

In early 1972, I was involved in laser research at Stanford Research Institute (now called SRI International) in Menlo Park, CA. At that time I was also circulating a proposal to obtain a small grant for some research in quantum biology. In that proposal I had raised the issue whether physical theory as we knew it was capable of describing life processes, and had suggested some measurements involving plants and lower organisms [3]. This proposal was widely circulated, and a copy was sent to Cleve Backster in New York City who was involved in measuring the electrical activity of plants with standard polygraph equipment. New York artist Ingo Swann chanced to see my proposal during a visit to Backster's lab, and wrote me suggesting that if I were interested in investigating the boundary between the physics of the animate and inanimate, I should consider experiments of the parapsychological type. Swann then went on to describe some apparently successful experiments in psychokinesis in which he had participated at Prof. Gertrude Schmeidler's laboratory at the City College of New York. As a result of this correspondence I invited him to visit SRI for a week in June 1972 to demonstrate such effects, frankly, as much out of personal scientific curiosity as anything else.

Prior to Swann's visit I arranged for access to a well-shielded magneto-meter used in a quark-detection experiment in the Physics Department at Stanford University. During our visit to this laboratory, sprung as a surprise to Swann, he appeared to perturb the operation of the magnetometer, located in a vault below the floor of the building and shielded by mu-metal shielding, an aluminum container, copper shielding and a superconducting shield. As if to add insult to injury, he then went on to "remote view" the interior of the apparatus, rendering by drawing a reasonable facsimile of its rather complex (and heretofore unpublished) construction. It was this latter feat that impressed me perhaps even more than the former, as it also eventually did representatives of the intelligence community. I wrote up these observations and circulated it among my scientific colleagues in draft form of what was eventually published as part of a conference proceeding [4].

In a few short weeks a pair of visitors showed up at SRI with the above report in hand. Their credentials showed them to be from the CIA. They knew of my previous background as a Naval Intelligence Officer and then civilian employee at the National Security Agency (NSA) several years earlier, and felt they could discuss their concerns with me openly. There was, they told me, increasing concern in the intelligence community about the level of effort in Soviet parapsychology being funded by the Soviet security services [5]; by Western scientific standards the field was considered nonsense by most working scientists. As a result they had been on the lookout for a research laboratory outside of academia that could handle a quiet, low-profile classified investigation, and SRI appeared to fit the bill. They asked if I could arrange an opportunity for them to carry out some simple experiments with Swann, and, if the tests proved satisfactory, would I consider a pilot program along these lines? I agreed to consider this, and arranged for the requested tests. [2]

The tests were simple, the visitors simply hiding objects in a box and asking Swann to attempt to describe the contents. The results generated in these experiments are perhaps captured most eloquently by the following example. In one test Swann said "I see something small, brown and irregular, sort of like a leaf or some-thing that resembles it, except that it seems very much alive, like it's even moving!" The target chosen by one of the visitors turned out to be a small live moth, which indeed did look like a leaf. Although not all responses were quite so precise, nonetheless the integrated results were sufficiently impressive that in short order an eight-month, $49,909 Biofield Measurements Program was negotiated as a pilot study, a laser colleague Russell Targ who had had a long-time interest and involvement in parapsychology joined the program, and the experimental effort was begun in earnest.

Early Remote Viewing Results

During the eight-month pilot study of remote viewing the effort gradually evolved from the remote viewing of symbols and objects in envelopes and boxes, to the remote viewing of local target sites in the San Francisco Bay area, demarked by outbound experimenters sent to the site under strict protocols devised to prevent artifactual results. Later judging of the results were similarly handled by double-blind protocols designed to foil artifactual matching. Since these results have been presented in detail elsewhere, both in the scientific literature [6-8] and in popular book format [9], I direct the interested reader to these sources. To summarize, over the years the back-and-forth criticism of protocols, refinement of methods, and successful replication of this type of remote viewing in independent laboratories [10-14], has yielded considerable scientific evidence for the reality of the phenomenon. Adding to the strength of these results was the discovery that a growing number of individuals could be found to demonstrate high-quality remote viewing, often to their own surprise, such as the talented Hella Hammid. As a separate issue, however, most convincing to our early program monitors were the results now to be described, generated under their own control.

First, during the collection of data for a formal remote viewing series targeting indoor laboratory apparatus and outdoor locations (a series eventually published in toto in the Proc. IEEE [7]), the CIA contract monitors, ever watchful for possible chicanery, participated as remote viewers themselves in order to critique the protocols. In this role three separate viewers, designated visitors V1 - V3 in the IEEE paper, contributed seven of the 55 viewings, several of striking quality. Reference to the IEEE paper for a comparison of descriptions/ drawings to pictures of the associated targets, generated by the contract monitors in their own viewings, leaves little doubt as to why the contract monitors came to the conclusion that there was something to remote viewing (see, for example, Figure 1 herein).

As summarized in the Executive Summary of the now-released Final Report [2] of the second year of the program, "The development of this capability at SRI has evolved to the point where visiting CIA personnel with no previous exposure to such concepts have performed well under controlled laboratory conditions (that is, generated target descriptions of sufficiently high quality to permit blind matching of descriptions to targets by independent judges)." What happened next, however, made even these results pale in comparison.

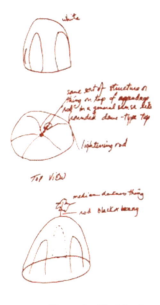

Figure 1 – Sketch of Target by VI

Figure 2 – Target (merry-go-round)

Coordinate Remote Viewing

To determine whether it was necessary to have a "beacon" individual at the target site, Swann suggested carrying out an experiment to remote view the planet Jupiter before the upcoming NASA Pioneer 10 fly by. In that case, much to his chagrin (and ours) he found a ring around Jupiter, and wondered if perhaps he had remote viewed Saturn by mistake. Our colleagues in astronomy were quite unimpressed as well, until the flyby revealed that an unanticipated ring did in fact exist. [3] Expanding the protocols yet further, Swann proposed a series of experiments in which the target was designated not by sending a "beacon" person to the target site, but rather by the use of geographical coordinates, latitude and longitude in degrees, minutes and seconds. Needless to say, this proposal seemed even more outrageous than "ordinary" remote viewing. The difficulties in taking this proposal seriously, designing protocols to eliminate the possibility of a combination of globe memorization and eidetic or photographic memory, and so forth, are discussed in considerable detail in Reference [9]. Suffice it to say that investigation of this approach, which we designated Scanate (scanning by coordinate), eventually provided us with sufficient evidence to bring it up to the contract monitors and suggest a test under their control. A description of that test and its results, carried out in mid-1973 during the initial pilot study, are best presented by quoting directly from the Executive Summary of the Final Report of the second year's follow-up program [2]. The remote viewers were Ingo Swann and Pat Price, and the entire transcripts are available in the released documents [2].

In order to subject the remote viewing phenomena to a rigorous long distance test under external control, a request for geographical coordinates of a site unknown to subject and experimenters was forwarded to the OSI group responsible for threat analysis in this area. In response, SRI personnel received a set of geographical coordinates (latitude and longitude in degrees, minutes, and seconds) of a facility, hereafter referred to as the West Virginia Site. The experimenters then carried out a remote viewing experiment on a double-blind basis, that is, blind to experimenters as well as subject. The experiment had as its goal the determination of the utility of remote viewing under conditions approximating an operational scenario. Two subjects targeted on the site, a sensitive installation. One subject drew a detailed map of the building and grounds layout, the other provided information about the interior including code words, data subsequently verified by sponsor sources (report available from COTR).[4]

Since details concerning the site's mission in general, [5] and evaluation of the remote viewing test in particular, remain highly classified to this day, all that can be said is that interest in the client community was heightened considerably following this exercise. Because Price found the above exercise so interesting, as a personal challenge he went on to scan the other side of the globe for a Communist Bloc equivalent and found one located in the Urals, the detailed description of which is also included in Ref. [2]. As with the West Virginia Site, the report for the Urals Site was also verified by personnel in the sponsor organization as being substantially correct.

What makes the West Virginia/Urals Sites viewings so remarkable is that these are not best-ever examples culled out of a longer list; these are literally the first two site-viewings carried out in a simulated operational-type scenario. In fact, for Price these were the very first two remote viewings in our program altogether, and he was invited to participate in yet further experimentation.

Operational Remote Viewing (Semipalatinsk, USSR)

Midway through the second year of the program (July 1974) our CIA sponsor decided to challenge us to provide data on a Soviet site of ongoing operational significance. Pat Price was the remote viewer. A description of the remote viewing, taken from our declassified final report [2], reads as given below. I cite this level of detail to indicate the thought that goes into such an "experiment" to minimize cueing while at the same time being responsive to the requirements of an operational situation. Again, this is not a "best-ever" example from a series of such viewings, but rather the very first operational Soviet target concerning which we were officially tasked. "To determine the utility of remote viewing under operational conditions, a long-distance remote viewing experiment was carried out on a sponsor designated target of current interest, an unidentified research center at Semipalatinsk, USSR.

This experiment, carried out in three phases, was under direct control of the COTR. To begin the experiment, the COTR furnished map coordinates in degrees, minutes and seconds. The only additional information provided was the designation of the target as an R&D test facility. The experimenters then closeted themselves with Subject S1, gave him the map coordinates and indicated the designation of the target as an R&D test facility. A remote-viewing experiment was then carried out. This activity constituted Phase I of the experiment.

Figure 3 shows the subject's graphic effort for building layout; Figure 4 shows the subject's particular attention to a multistory gantry crane he observed at the site. Both results were obtained by the experimenters on a double-blind basis before exposure to any additional COTR-held information, thus eliminating the possibility of cueing. These results were turned over to the client representatives for evaluation. For comparison, an artist's rendering of the site as known to the COTR (but not to the experimenters until later) is shown in Figure 5.

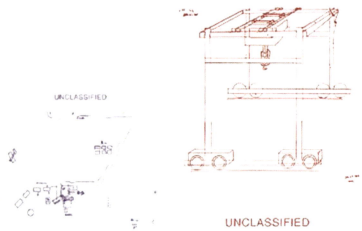

Figure 3 - Subject effort
at building layout

UNCLASSIFIED
Figure 4 - Subject effort
construction crane

Were the results not promising, the experiment would have stopped at this point. Description of the multistory crane, however, a relatively unusual target item, was taken as indicative of possible target acquisition. Therefore, Phase II was begun, defined by the subject being made "witting" (of the client) by client representatives who introduced themselves to the subject at that point; Phase II also included a second round of experimentation on the Semipalatinsk site with direct participation of client representatives in which further data were obtained and evaluated. As preparation for this phase, client representatives purposely kept themselves blind to all but general knowledge of the target site to minimize the possibility of cueing. The Phase II effort was focused on the generation of physical data that could be independently verified by other client sources, thus providing a calibration of the process.

The end of Phase II gradually evolved into the first part of Phase III, the generation of unverifiable data concerning the

Semipalatinsk site not available to the client, but of operational interest nonetheless. Several hours of tape transcript and a notebook of drawings were generated over a two-week period.

The data describing the Semipalatinsk site were evaluated by the sponsor, and are contained in a separate report. In general, several details concerning the salient technology of the Semipalatinsk site appeared to dovetail with data from other sources, and a number of specific large structural elements were correctly described. The results contained noise along with the signal, but were nonetheless clearly differentiated from the chance results that were generated by control subjects in comparison experiments carried out by the COTR."

For discussion of the ambiance and personal factors involved in carrying out this experiment, along with further detail generated as Price (see Figure 6) "roamed" the facility, including detailed comparison of Price's RV-generated information with later determined "ground-truth reality," see the accompanying article by Russell Targ in the Journal of Scientific Exploration <http:// www. jse.com/>, Vol. 10, No. 1.

Additional experiments having implications for intelligence concerns were carried out, such as the remote viewing of cipher machine type apparatus, and the RV-sorting of sealed envelopes to differentiate those that contained letters with secret writing from those that did not. To discuss these here in detail would take us too far afield, but the interested reader can follow up by referring to the now-declassified project documents [2].

Figure 5 - Actual COTR rendering of Semipalatinsk, USSR target site.

Follow-on Programs

The above discussion brings us up to the end of 1975. As a result of the material being generated by both SRI and CIA remote viewers, interest in the program in government circles, especially within the intelligence community, intensified considerably and led to an ever increasing briefing schedule. This in turn led to an ever-increasing number of clients, contracts and tasking, and therefore expansion of the program to a multi-client base, and eventually to an integrated joint-services program under single-agency (DIA)[6] leadership. To meet the demand for the increased level of effort we first increased our professional staff by inviting Ed May to join the program in 1976, then screened and added to the program a cadre of remote viewers as consultants, and let subcontracts to increase our scope of activity.

As the program expanded, in only a very few cases could the client's identities and program tasking be revealed. Examples include a NASA-funded study negotiated early in the program by Russ Targ to determine whether the internal state of an electronic random-number-generator could be detected by RV processes [16], and a study funded by the Naval Electronics Systems Command to determine whether attempted remote viewing of distant light flashes would induce correlated changes in the viewer's brainwave (EEG) production [17]. For essentially all other projects, during my 14-yr. tenure at SRI, however, the identity of the clients and most of the tasking were classified and remain so today. (The exception was the occasional privately funded study.) We are told, however, that further declassification and release of much of this material is almost certain to occur.

What can be said, then, about further development of the program in the two decades following 1975?[7] In broad terms it can be said that much of the SRI effort was directed not so much toward developing an operational U.S. capability, but rather toward assessing the threat potential of its use against the U.S. by others. The words 'threat assessment' were often used to describe the program's purpose during its development, especially during the early years. As a result, much of the remote-viewing activity was carried out under conditions where ground-truth reality was a priori known or could be determined, such as the description of U.S. facilities and technological developments, the timing of rocket test firings and underground nuclear tests, and the location of individuals and mobile units. And, of course, we were responsive to requests to provide assistance during such events as the loss of an airplane or the taking of hostages, relying on the talents of an increasing cadre of remote-viewer/ consultants, some well-known in the field such as Keith Harary, and many who have not surfaced publicly until recently, such as Joe McMoneagle

Figure 6 - Left to right: Christopher Green,[25] Pat Price,[26] and Hal Puthoff.
Picture taken following a successful experiment involving glider-ground RV.

One might ask whether in this program RV-generated information was ever of sufficient significance as to influence decisions at a policy level. This is of course impossible to determine unless policymakers were to come forward with a statement in the affirmative. One example of a possible candidate is a study we performed at SRI during the Carter administration debates concerning proposed deployment of the mobile MX missile system.

---

[25] Dr. Christopher Green MD. Neurophysiology, received the CIA's National Intelligence Medal as a Scientific Advisory Board Member to the CIA's Directorate of Intelligence.

[26] One of the finest remote viewers ever, Pat Price, a former police commissioner and councilman in Burbank, CA, came to the Government's attention when he viewed officers, interiors, and files at the virtually unknown, nuclear hardened Naval Satellite Intelligence site in West Virginia. When the Pentagon was shown the data, Price was interrogated by the U.S. Defense Investigative Service who demanded to know who had breached security and how they did it. He is reputed to be the only viewer that could read numbers and letters on a target. Later he viewed inside the Soviet installation at Mount Narodnaya in the Ural Mountains. He went on to work for the CIA and is reputed to have died of a heart attack in July of 1975, in Las Vegas. Even though he was supposedly dead on arrival at the hospital, no autopsy was performed. Suspicions have always existed about the truth of his death. [author]

In that scenario missiles were to be randomly shuffled from silo to silo in a silo field, in a form of high-tech shell game. In a computer simulation of a twenty-silo field with randomly-assigned (hidden) missile locations, we were able, using RV-generated data, to show rather forcefully that the application of a sophisticated statistical averaging technique (sequential sampling) could in principle permit an adversary to defeat the system. I briefed these results to the appropriate offices at their request, and a written report with the technical details was widely circulated among groups responsible for threat analysis [18], and with some impact. What role, if any, our small contribution played in the mix of factors behind the enormously complex decision to cancel the program will probably never be known, and must of course a priori be considered in all likelihood negligible. Nonetheless, this is a prototypical example of the kind of tasking that by its nature potentially had policy implications.

Even though the details of the broad range of experiments, some brilliant successes, many total failures, have not yet been released, we have nonetheless been able to publish summaries of what was learned in these studies about the overall characteristics of remote viewing, as in Table 5 of Reference [8]. Furthermore, over the years we were able to address certain questions of scientific interest in a rigorous way and to publish the results in the open literature. Examples include the apparent lack of attenuation of remote viewing due to seawater shielding (submersible experiments) [8], the amplification of RV performance by use of error-correcting coding techniques [19, 20], and the utility of a technique we call associational remote viewing (ARV) to generate useful predictive information [21].8

As a sociological aside, we note that the overall efficacy of remote viewing in a program like this was not just a scientific issue. For example, when the Semipalatinsk data described earlier was forwarded for analysis, one group declined to get involved because the whole concept was unscientific nonsense, while a second group declined because, even though it might be real, it was possibly demonic; a third group had to be found. And, as in the case of public debate about such phenomena, the program's image was on occasion as likely to be damaged by an over enthusiastic supporter, as by a detractor. Personalities, politics and personal biases were always factors to be dealt with.

Official Statements/Perspectives

With regard to admission by the government of its use of remote viewers under operational conditions, officials have on occasion been relatively forthcoming. President Carter, in a speech to college students in Atlanta in September 1995, is quoted by Reuters as saying that during his administration a plane went down in Zaire, and a meticulous sweep of the African terrain by American spy satellites failed to locate any sign of the wreckage. It was then "without my knowledge" that the head of the CIA (Adm. Stansfield Turner) turned to a woman reputed to have psychic powers. As told by Carter, "she gave some latitude and longitude figures. We focused our satellite cameras on that point and the plane was there." Independently, Turner himself also has admitted the Agency's use of a remote viewer (in this case, Pat Price).[9] And recently, in a segment taped for the British television series Equinox [22], Maj. Gen. Ed Thompson, Assistant Chief of Staff for Intelligence, U.S. Army (1977-1981), volunteered "I had one or more briefings by SRI and was impressed.... The decision I made was to set up a small, in-house, low-cost effort in remote viewing...

Finally, a recent unclassified report [23] prepared for the CIA by the American Institutes for Research (AIR), concerning a remote viewing effort carried out under a DIA program called Star Gate (discussed in detail elsewhere in this volume), cites the roles of the CIA and DIA in the history of the program, including acknowledgment that a cadre of full-time government employees used remote viewing techniques to respond to tasking from operational military organizations. [10]

As information concerning the various programs spawned by intelligence-community interest is released, and the dialog concerning their scientific and social significance is joined, the results are certain to be hotly debated. Bearing witness to this fact are the companion articles in this volume by Ed May, Director of the SRI and SAIC programs since 1985, and by Jessica Utts and Ray Hyman, consultants on the AIR evaluation cited above. These articles address in part the AIR study. That study, limited in scope to a small fragment of the overall program effort, resulted in a conclusion that although laboratory research showed statistically significant results, use of remote viewing in intelligence gathering was not warranted.

Evidential Details

Regardless of one's a priori position, however, an unimpassioned observer cannot help but attest to the following fact. Despite the ambiguities inherent in the type of exploration covered in these programs, the integrated results appear to provide unequivocal evidence of a human capacity to access events remote in space and time, however falteringly, by some cognitive process not yet understood. My years of involvement as a research manager in these programs have left me with the conviction that this fact must be taken into account in any attempt to develop an unbiased picture of the structure of reality.

Footnotes

1 - One example being the release of documents that are the subject of this report - see the memoir by Russell Targ.

2 - Since the reputation of the intelligence services is mixed among members of the general populace, I have on occasion been challenged as to why I would agree to cooperate with the CIA or other elements of the intelligence community in this work. My answer is simply that as a result of my own previous exposure to this community I became persuaded that war can almost always be traced to a failure in intelligence, and that therefore the strongest weapon for peace is good intelligence.

3 - This result was published by us in advance of the ring's discovery [9].

4 - Editor's footnote added here: COTR - Contracting Officer's Technical Representative.

5 - An NSA listening post at the Navy's Sugar Grove facility, according to intelligence-community chronicler Bamford [15]

6 - DIA - Defense Intelligence Agency. The CIA dropped out as a major player in the mid-seventies due to pressure on the Agency (unrelated to the RV Program) from the Church-Pike Congressional Committee.

7 - See also the contribution by Ed May elsewhere in this volume concerning his experiences from 1985 on during his tenure as Director.

8 - For example, one application of this technique yielded not only a published, statistically significant result, but also a return of $26,000 in 30 days in the silver futures market [21].

9 - The direct quote is given in Targ's contribution elsewhere in this volume.

10 - "From 1986 to the first quarter of FY 1995, the DoD para-normal psychology program received more than 200 tasks from operational military organizations requesting that the program staff apply a paranormal psychological technique know (sic) as "remote viewing" (RV) to attain information unavailable from other sources."[23]

References

[1] "CIA Statement on 'Remote Viewing," CIA Public Affairs Office, 6 September 1995.

[2] Harold E. Puthoff and Russell Targ, "Perceptual Augmentation Techniques," SRI Progress Report No. 3 (31 Oct. 1974) and Final Report (1 Dec. 1975) to the CIA, covering the period January 1974 through February 1975, the second year of the program. This effort was funded at the level of $149,555.

[3] H. E. Puthoff, "Toward a Quantum Theory of Life Process," unpubl proposal, Stanford Research Institute (1972).

[4] H. E. Puthoff and R. Targ, "Physics, Entropy and Psychokine-sis," in Proc. Conf. Quantum Physics and Parapsychology (Gen-eva, Switzerland); (New York: Parapsychology Foundation, 1975).

[5] Documented in "Paraphysics R&D - Warsaw Pact (U)," DST-1810S-202-78, Defense Intelligence Agency (30 March 1978).

[6] R. Targ and H. E. Puthoff, "Information Transfer under Conditions of Sensory Shielding," Nature 252, 602 (1974).

[7] H. E. Puthoff and R. Targ, "A Perceptual Channel for Information Transfer over Kilometer Distances: Historical Perspective and Recent Research," Proc. IEEE 64, 329 (1976).

[8] H. E. Puthoff, R. Targ and E. C. May, "Experimental Psi Research: Implications for Physics," in The Role of Consciousness in the Physical World", edited by R. G. Jahn (AAAS Selected Symposium 57, Westview Press, Boulder, 1981).

[9] R. Targ and H. E. Puthoff, Mind Reach (Delacorte Press, New York, 1977).

[10] J. P. Bisaha and B. J. Dunne, "Multiple Subject and Long-Distance Precognitive Remote Viewing of Geographical Locations," in Mind at Large, edited by C. T. Tart, H. E. Puthoff and R. Targ (Praeger, New York, 1979), p. 107.

[11] B. J. Dunne and J. P. Bisaha, "Precognitive Remote Viewing in the Chicago Area: a Replication of the Stanford Experiment," J. Parapsychology 43, 17 (1979).

[12] R. G. Jahn, "The Persistent Paradox of Psychic Phenomena: An Engineering Perspective," Proc. IEEE 70, 136 (1982).

[13] R. G. Jahn and B. J. Dunne, "On the Quantum Mechanics of Consciousness with Application to Anomalous Phenomena," Found. Phys. 16, 721 (1986).

[14] R. G. Jahn and B. J. Dunne, Margins of Reality (Harcourt, Brace and Jovanovich, New York, 1987).

[15] J. Bamford, The Puzzle Palace (Penguin Books, New York, 1983) pp. 218-222.

[16] R. Targ, P. Cole and H. E. Puthoff, "Techniques to Enhance Man/ Machine Communication," Stanford Research Institute Final Report on NASA Project NAS7-100 (August 1974).

[17] R. Targ, E. C. May, H. E. Puthoff, D. Galin and R. Ornstein, "Sensing of Remote EM Sources (Physiological Correlates)," SRI Intern'l Final Report on Naval Electronics Systems Command Project N00039-76-C-0077, covering the period November 1975 - to October 1976 (April 1978).

[18] H. E. Puthoff, "Feasibility Study on the Vulnerability of the MPS System to RV Detection Techniques," SRI Internal Report, 15 April 1979; revised 2 May 1979.

[19] H. E. Puthoff, "Calculator-Assisted Psi Amplification," Research in Parapsychology 1984, edited by Rhea White and J. Solfvin (Scarecrow Press, Metuchen, NJ, 1985), p. 48.

[20] H. E. Puthoff, "Calculator-Assisted Psi Amplification II: Use of the Sequential-Sampling Technique as a Variable-Length Majority-Vote Code," Research in Parapsychology 1985, edited by D. Weiner and D. Radin (Scarecrow Press, Metuchen, NJ, 1986), p. 73.

[21] H. E. Puthoff, "ARV (Associational Remote Viewing) Applications," Research in Parapsychology 1984, edited by Rhea White and J. Solfvin (Scarecrow Press, Metuchen, NJ, 1985), p. 121.

[22] "The Real X-Files", Independent Channel 4, England (27 August 1995); to be shown in the U.S. on the Discovery Channel.

[23] M. D. Mumford, A. M. Rose and D. Goslin, "An Evaluation of Remote Viewing: Research and Applications", American Institutes for Research (September 29, 1995). Copyright 1996 by Dr. H.E. Puthoff.

Targeted Reading

This catalogue was compiled to help people search for media from members of the military program.

McMoneagle, Joseph W.
- *Mind Trek;* Hampton Roads, 1993
- *The Ultimate Time Machine*; Hampton Roads, 1998
- *Remote Viewing Secrets*; Hampton Roads, 2000
- *The Stargate Chronicles*; Hampton Roads, 2002
- *Memoirs of a Psychic Spy: The Remarkable Life of U. S. Government Remote Viewer 001*; Hampton Roads, 2006

Buchanan, Leonard
- *The Seventh Sense – The Secrets of Remote Viewing as Told by a "Psychic Spy" for the U.S. Military*; Paraview Pocket Books, 2003
- *Remote Viewing Methods - Remote Viewing and Remote Influencing*; DVD, 2004

Smith, Paul H.
- *Reading the Enemy's Mind - Inside Stargate - America's Psychic Espionage Program*; Tor non-fiction, 2005

Morehouse, David A.
- *Psychic Warrior – Inside the CIA's Stargate Program: The True Story of a Soldiers Espionage and Awakening*; St Martin's Press, 1996
- *Nonlethal Weapons: War Without Death;* Praeger Publishers, 1996
- *Remote Viewing: The Complete User's Manual for Coordinate Remote Viewing*; Sounds True Publishers, 2011

Atwater, F. Holmes
- *Captain of My Ship, Master of My Soul: Living with Guidance;* Hampton Roads Publishing, 2001 with Puthoff, Harold E. and Targ, Russell

- *Mind Reach - Scientists Look at Psychic Abilities*; Delacorte,
  1977 & New World Library, 2004

Swann, Ingo
- *To Kiss the Earth Goodbye;* Hawthorne, New York, 1975
- *Star Fire,* Dell non-fiction, 1978
- *Everybody's Guide to Natural ESP: Unlocking the Extrasensory
  Power of Your Mind;* Jeremy P. Tharcher Imprint, 1991
- *Your Nostradamus Factor;* Fireside Press, 1993
- *Remote Viewing & ESP from the Inside Ou*t; DVD

Targ, Russell
- *Mind Race: Understanding and Using Psychic Abilities*, with Keith
  Harary; Ballantine Books, 1984
- *Miracles of Mind: Exploring Nonlocal Consciousness and
  Spiritual Healing*; New World Library, 1999
- *Limitless Mind: A Guide to Remote Viewing and Transformation
  of Consciousness*; New World Library, 2004

Other Resources

- Schnabel, Jim – *Remote Viewers: The Secret History of
  America's Psychic Spies*; Dell–non-fiction, 1997

- McRae, Ronald – *Mind Wars: The true story of Government
  Research into the Military Potential of Psychic Weapons*; St
  Martin's Press, 1984

- Gruber, Elmar – *Psychic Wars – Parapsychology in Espionage –
  and Beyond*; Blandford, London, 1999

- Moreno, Jonathon D. – *Mind Wars: Brain Science and the
  Military in the 21st Century*; Bellevue Literary Press, 2012

- Radin, Dean - *Entangled Minds: Extrasensory Experiences in a
  Quantum Reality*, Paraview Pocket Books, 2006

- Brown, Courtney - *Remote Viewing* - Farsight Press, 2005

- Dong, Paul with Thomas Rafill – *China's Super Psychics*; Marlowe
  & Co., New York, 1997

Additional Taskings

Lae City Airport, New Guinea - July, 1937 – This is the rumored Military intelligence report. Get into the cockpit for the last flight of the vanished pilot **Amelia Earhart**. The book includes a realignment of data culminating in a major reinterpretation of her radio messages. Learn of the plane's actual flight trajectory, cockpit dynamics, and her final thoughts. This unprecedented research, drawing on seven separate specialist organization's data, has never been brought forward before. The book includes a Pentagon quality debris field map with yardages and points of reference. It also exposés the Castaways Theory failures. When you make a decision you want to know what happened to Amelia Earhart, this is the data the Pentagon would have used to send naval air to recover the airplane. Awarded 5 stars from *GoodReads.com*

Ötzal Alps - Italian-Austrian border ~ 3,300 BC – Follow the trail of Europe's archeological "show of the century." Learn the whereabouts of **Ötzi the Iceman**'s unknown home camp and why and how he died alone in the mountains which some mistakenly regard as a Neolithic crime scene. The book includes remote viewing maps, pre-death tool drawings - including an undiscovered tool - his cabin, and the world's only real time portrait considered significant enough that the Museum in Bolzano, Italy requested it for Ötzi's 20th Anniversary exhibit. Interwoven with scientific quotation, this account also includes specifics of his tribal life in a now identified valley. This is the only book providing Ötzi's previously unknown course through the mountains using modern Alpine trail numbers. Learn the cause for his violent death which is the only solution that unifies the various theories.

Onboard RMS Titanic - North Atlantic - April, 1912 – In the first book to appear after the 2nd Officer's granddaughter's revelations, review the Evidential Details detailing what really happened in the crows nest as *Titanic* bore down on the ice. Then, move to a resolution regarding **Captain E. J. Smith**'s final actions in his previously unknown non-drowning death. The book includes obscure artifact drawings whose existence was only confirmed through ocean floor salvage after the remote viewing sessions. Once the last lifeboat was away the Captain knew mass death was imminent. Read History's only account of those last 20 minutes as the ship was set to take over 1520 scared to death passengers down into the frigid black ocean at 2:18 in the morning.

Civil War Special, State of Maryland - September, 1862 – Considered an unsolvable whodunit, this little known, but most significant mystery in America's Civil War resolves who lost Confederate **General Robert E. Lee**'s top secret *Special Order 191*. The result was the battles of South Mountain and Harper's Ferry, leading directly to the bloodiest day in American History at Antietam Creek. The upshot was the timing of the Emancipation Proclamation. With information from the National Park Service, the book provides the unknown aerial campground maps and reveals the previously unknown who, why, when, where and how these orders found their way into the Union Theater Commander's hands. This book also provides the world's first clinical determination on Union General George McClellan's psychological problems.

Last Stand Hill - Little Big Horn Battlefield, Montana - June, 1876 – This is History's only view of **General George Armstrong Custer**'s last stand from the victors and the vanquished perspectives. Read about Chief Sitting Bull's and Custer's battle thoughts. Learn of his true cause of Custer's death and the amazing reasons his body is likely not in his tomb at West Point. You get new remote viewing generated battle maps with a drawing of Custer's last fighting stance, a near death facial close-up drawing and, since he was never photographed, the world's only full page color portrait of Indian War Chief *Crazy Horse*.

Each book is designed to be everything you'll need to know about the resolution of a particular mystery.

Princess Diana References

[i] McMoneagle, Joseph W., *Remote Viewing Secrets – A Handbook*; Hampton Roads Publishing Company, Inc. 2000 p. xv

[ii] McMoneagle, Joseph W., *The Stargate Chronicles*; Hampton Roads Publishing Company, Inc. 2002 p. 182

[iii] Simmons, Simone, *Diana – The Secret Years* with Susan Hill; Ballantine Books 1998 p.120

[iv] Delorm, Rene, *Diana & Dodi - A Love Story - By the Butler Who Saw Their Romance Blossom*, with Barry Fox and Nadine Taylor; Tallfellow Press 1998, p.144

[v] Anderson, Christopher, *The Day Diana Died;* William Morrow and Company 1998 p.114

[vi] Anderson; p.113

[vii] Delorm; p.154

[viii] ibid; p.154

[ix] The Learning Channel Presentation - *Princess Diana*; A Fulcrum Production; a Granada Presentation for ITV 1998; hereafter referred to as *TLC*

[x] Delorm; p.155

[xi] Anderson; p.99

[xii] ibid; p.166

[xiii] Sancton, Thomas and Scott MacLeod, *Death of a Princess - The Investigation*; St. Martin's Press 1998 p.157

[xiv] Delorm; p.157

[xv] ibid; p.158

[xvi] Spoto, Donald, *Diana - The Last Year;*; Harmony Books 1997 p. 171

[xvii] Sanction; p.158-9

[xviii] TLC - Mohammed Al-Fayed interview

[xix] Junor, Penny, *Charles - Victim or Villain*; Harper Collins Publishers 1998; p.18

[xx] Sanction; p.167

[xxi] Final Report - Paris Prosecutor's Office; Head of the Prosecution Department at Courts of the First Instance; Examining Magistrates Hervé Stephan and Christine Devidal

[xxii] *TLC* - documentary information

[xxiii] *TLC* - interview with Dr. Martin Skinner.

[xxiv] Anderson; p.191

[xxv] Interview with Mohammed Al Fayed as per his internet site address: www.alfayed.com/indexie4.html, as published to the Internet on October 25, 1998

[xxvi] Spoto; p.172

[xxvii] Sanction; p 251

[xxviii] ibid; p. 6

[xxix] *Newsweek* Magazine; September 8, 1997; p. 33

[xxx] ibid; p. 241

[xxxi] Buchanan, Lyn, *The Seventh Sense*, Paraview Pocket Books, 2003, p. 190

[xxxii] Sanction; p. 17

[xxxiii] ibid; p.17 - 18

[xxxiv] Junor; p. 20

[xxxv] Spoto; p.180

[xxxvi] Junor; p. 22

[xxxvii] *French Final Accident Report* – Conclusionary Statement section

[xxxviii] New York Times; December 15, 2008

Joan of Arc References

[xxxix] Claudel, Paul, *Cahiers du Rhone*; 1942; p. 2

[xl] Pernoud, Regine, *Joan of Arc - By Herself and Her Witnesses*; Stein and Day Publishers 1962; p. 16

[xli] TOR; testimony of Dame Marguerite La Touroulde

[xlii] Testimony of Catherine, wife of Leroyer. Trial of Rehabilitation of Joan of Arc 1455-6 (*Proces de condamnation et de rehabilitation de Jeanne d'Arc, dite la Pucelle*, Paris 1841-1849; translated by Jules Quicherat) p. 199; translated from Old French to Latin and subsequently 'authenticated' by notaries. Of five originnal copies three survive. One in the French Library of National Assembly; two others at the Bibliotheque Nationale, hereafter referred to as TOR.

[xliii] TOR; Testimony of Messire Jean Lefumeux

[xliv] TOR; Sieur De Gaucourt testimony

[xlv] TOR; testimony of Husson Le Maitre

[xlvi] Clin, Marie Veronique and Pernoud, Regine, *Joans Report to Friar Jean Pasuerel in Joan of Arc Her Story*; St Martins Press 1998; p. 23

[xlvii] Duparc, Pierre, *La Deliverance d'Orleans et la mission de Jeanne d'Arc* in *Jeanne d'Arc: Une epoque, un rayonnement*; Paris, 1982; the testimony of Sequin in the rehabilitation trial - I:472; TOR; Testimony of Brother Seguin De Seguin

[xlviii] Quicherat, Jules, Pius II, *Commentari verum memorabilium quae temporibus suis contingerunt*, IV: 510 Paris.

[xlix] DuPuy, R. Ernest and Trevor N., *The Encyclopedia of Military History from 3,500 B.C. to the Present,* revised edition; Harper & Row Publishers, 1977; p.416

[l] Devries, Kelly, *Joan of Arc – A Military Leader;* Sutton Publishing; 1999 - The original letter is no longer in existence. Its full text can be found in this book.

[li] TOR; Testimony of Simon Baucroix, Squire

[lii] *DuPuy*; p. 417

[liii] Quicherat - *Histoire du siege d'Orleans et des bonneurs rendus a la Pucelle*,1854

[liv] Quicherat, IV:440-7 *Chronique de ducs Bourgogne* by George Chastellain

[lv] *Pernoud;* p. 161

[lvi] ibid; p. 213

[lvii] TOR in *Pernoud*; p. 162

[lviii] Trial of Condemnation of Joan of Arc 1431; (*Proces de condamnation et de rehabilitation de Jeanne d'Arc, dite la Pucelle*, Paris 1841-1849; translated by Jules Quicherat), hereafter referred to as TOC (*Pernoud*; p. 181)

[lix] *TOC* (*Pernoud*; p. 181)

[lx] *TOR; p. 211* (*Pernoud*; p. 183)

[lxi] *TOC;* (Pernoud; p. 186)

[lxii] *Pernoud*; p. 206

[lxiii] *TOR p. 187;* Testimony of Knight Haimond de Macy; (*Pernoud* p. 208)

[lxiv] *TOR* p. 227 – 228; Testimony by Jean Massieu (*Pernoud* ; p. 212)

[lxv] *Pernoud*; p. 217-5

[lxvi] *TOR* p. 268 ; Testimony by Isambart de la Pierre (*Pernoud*; p. 220)

[lxvii] *TOC* p. 395 - 399

[lxviii] *TOR* p. 268; Testimony of Isambart de la Pierre (*Pernoud* ; p. 222); p. 234-5

[lxix] *Pernoud;* p. 233

[lxx] Sackvill-West Nicolson - *Saint Joan of Arc*; Country Life Press 1936;p. 341

[lxxi] *TOC*; Pernoud p. 230

[lxxii] *TOR*; statement of Jean Massieu; (*Pernoud*; p. 231)

[lxxiii] *Pernoud*; p. 199

[lxxiv] Freud, Sigmund, *Civilization and it's Discontents;* Chapter 7

[lxxv] *DuPuy*; p. 417

[lxxvi] *Devries*; p. 7

Made in United States
Orlando, FL
23 August 2025

64230981R10083